Infant/Toddler Caregiu

A Guide to
Culturally
Sensitive Care

Second Edition

Edited by

Elita Amini Virmani and Peter L. Mangione

Developed collaboratively by the

California Department of Education

and WestEd

  WestEd

Publishing Information

Infant/Toddler Caregiving: A Guide to Culturally Sensitive Care, Second Edition, was developed by WestEd, San Francisco. The publication was edited by Faye Ong, working in cooperation with Elita Amini Virmani and Peter Mangione, WestEd; and Sy Dang Nguyen, Consultant, Child Development Division, California Department of Education (CDE). It was prepared for printing by Tuyet Truong, with the cover and interior design created by Juan D. Sanchez. The document was published by the California Department of Education, 1430 N Street, Sacramento, CA 95814-5901. It was distributed under the provisions of the Library Distribution Act and *Government Code* Section 11096.

ISBN 978-0-8011-1734-3

Ordering Information

Copies of this publication are available for purchase from the California Department of Education (CDE). For prices and ordering information, visit http://www.cde.ca.gov/re/pn/rc/ or call the CDE Press sales office at 1-800-995-4099.

Notice

The guidance in *Infant/Toddler Caregiving: A Guide to Culturally Sensitive Care, Second Edition,* is not binding on local educational agencies or other entities. Except for statutes, regulations, and court decisions referenced herein, the document is exemplary, and compliance with it is not mandatory. (See *Education Code* Section 33308.5.)

Prepared for printing
by CSEA members

Contents

A Message from the State Superintendent of Public Instruction   vi

Acknowledgments   vii

About the Authors   x

Introduction   xi

Section One: Understanding the Social Context of Infant/Toddler Care   1

Chapter 1. Culture and Identity Development: Getting Infants and
Toddlers Off to a Great Start   2
  Carol Brunson Day
The Beginnings of Identity Development Are in Infancy   2
Dimensions of Identity Development   3
The Role of Culture in Development   4
Cultural Empowerment: Preparing Infant/Toddler Care Teachers for
  Competent Practice   5
Culture as a Process   6
Culturally Responsive Practices That Support Identity Development   8
References   10

Chapter 2. Prejudice, Bias, and Inequity in the Lives of Infants and Toddlers   13
  Louise Derman-Sparks
Societal Inequity and Families   14
What Infants and Toddlers See and Hear in Child Care Settings   14
Socialization in Two Cultures   16
Practicing Culturally Responsive Care   17
Building Blocks of a Culturally Responsive Care/Learning Environment   19
Conclusion   22
Glossary   23
References   24

Chapter 3. Inclusion of Children with Special Needs in Diverse Early
Care Settings   25
  Deborah Chen
Diverse Perspectives on Disability   25
Differences in Perspectives   27
Understanding Early Intervention Terminology, Eligibility, and Intervention   28
Eligibility for Early Intervention Services   28
Initiating the Early Intervention Process: Making Referrals   29

Individualized Family Service Plan   33
Teaming with Interpreters   33
Gathering Information from Families   34
Sharing Information with Families   36
Supporting Participation and a Sense of Belonging in the Early Care Setting   36
Person-First Language   37
Universal Design for Learning   37
Teaming with Early Intervention Service Providers   38
Embedding Specific Learning Opportunities in Daily Routines   38
Questions to Guide Practice   39
Conclusion   39
References   40

Section Two: Becoming Informed About Cultural Practices and Cultural Communities   41

Chapter 4. A Cultural Communities and Cultural Practices Approach to
Understanding Infant and Toddler Care   42
Alison Wishard Guerra and Sarah Garrity
Participation in Cultural Practices at Home and in the Early Care Setting   44
Understanding Cultural Communities   45
Understanding Cultural Practices   47
Families and Communities   47
Interactions with Children and Families and Becoming Informed About Cultural
Practices and Cultural Communities   51
Understanding the Classroom or Program as Its Own Cultural Community   52
References   53

Chapter 5. Cultural Sensitivity in Caregiving Routines: The Essential Activities
of Daily Living   56
Janet Gonzalez-Mena
Differing Beliefs and Values   56
What Is a Routine?   57
Cultural Differences in Daily Routines: Toileting, Feeding,
and Sleeping/Napping   58
Toileting   59
Feeding Practices   61
Sleeping/Napping Routines   63
Summary   64
References   65

Section Three: Creating Collaborative, Reciprocal Relationships with Linguistically Diverse Families   67

Chapter 6. Developing Culturally Responsive Caregiving Practices: Acknowledge,
Ask, and Adapt   68
Louise Derman-Sparks
The Process of Culturally Responsive Care   68

Acknowledge, Ask, and Adapt   72
Identifying Culturally Responsive and Culturally Insensitive Practices   75
Scenario 1: A Baby Crying   76
Scenario 2: Babies Wearing Protective Amulets   79
Scenario 3: Babies Staying Clean or Engaging in Active Learning   82
Scenario 4: "Two Mommies"   84
Developmental Issues or Cultural Differences?   86
Determining the Nature of the Behavior   86
Conclusion   88
References   88
Thinking/Doing Activity 1   89
Thinking/Doing Activity 2   90
Thinking/Doing Activity 3   91
Thinking/Doing Activity 4   92
Thinking/Doing Activity 5   93
Thinking Doing Activity 6   94

Chapter 7. Creating Collaborative, Reciprocal Relationships with Linguistically
Diverse Families   95
    Gisela Jia and Alison Wishard Guerra
Linguistic and Cultural Diversity at Home   95
Family Beliefs and Goals for Children's Bicultural and Bilingual
    Development   96
The Importance of Developing Home Language and Cultural Competence   97
Communication and Language Development in Non-English-Speaking
    Homes   97
Strategies for Creating Collaborative, Reciprocal Relationships with Linguistically
    Diverse Families   98
Conclusion   104
References   105

Section Four: Suggested Resources   107

A Message from the State Superintendent of Public Instruction

Culturally responsive practices are essential to supporting children's development in all domains. To address culturally responsive practices in early care settings, seven noted experts have been brought together to create this second edition of *A Guide to Culturally Sensitive Care,* which was developed collaboratively by the California Department of Education and WestEd. The guide focuses on understanding the role that culture and language play in contributing to children's development and includes important considerations in caring for young children from diverse cultural and linguistic backgrounds. The publication introduces readers to new ways of thinking about culture and its impact on child development. It suggests ways for teachers to collaborate with families to better understand how family goals and values influence their daily caregiving practices and routines. In addition, the book aims to help infant/toddler care teachers deepen their appreciation of how they are influenced by their own cultural beliefs and how an awareness of one's beliefs is the foundation for being responsive to the cultural perspectives and experiences of young children and families. Above all, this resource offers infant/toddler care teachers many practical ideas on how to create relationships with families and establish meaningful connections between the home and the early care setting.

It is our hope that everyone in the infant/toddler field will use this new publication hand in hand with the other resources created by the Department of Education to promote the well-being and long-term development of California's youngest children and their families.

Tom Torlakson

TOM TORLAKSON
State Superintendent of Public Instruction

Acknowledgments

The first edition of this publication was developed by the WestEd Center for Child and Family Studies, under the direction of J. Ronald Lally. Funding for the first edition was generously provided by the Carnegie Corporation of New York. Special thanks go to J. Ronald Lally, Jesus Cortez, Louise Derman-Sparks, Janet Gonzales-Mena, Alicia F. Lieberman, Jayanthi Mistri, Carol Brunson Day, Carol Lou Young-Holt, and Peter L. Mangione for their contributions to the first edition; to Karla Nygaard for editorial assistance; and to Robert Cervantes, Kay Witcher, Janet Poole, Virginia Benson, Helen Nguyen, and Mary Smithberger, Child Development Division, California Department of Education, for their review of the content. Thanks are also extended to the members of the national and the California review panels and the Advisory Panel for Culturally Sensitive Care for their comments and suggestions. The national panel members were T. Berry Brazelton, Laura Dittman, Richard Fiene, Magda Gerber, Asa Hilliard, Alice Honig, Jeree Pawl, Sally Provence, Eleanor Szanton, Yolanda Torres, Bernice Weissbourd, and Donna Wittmer. The California panel members were Dorlene Clayton, Dee Cuney, Ronda Garcia, Jacquelyne Jackson, Lee McKay, Janet Nielsen, Pearlene Reese, Maria Ruiz, June Sale, Patty Siegel, and Lenore Thompson. The members of the culturally sensitive care panel were Ruby Burgess, Jesus Cortez, Louise Derman-Sparks, Ron Henderson, Frances E. Kendall, Christina Guzman-Pederson, Carol Brunson Day, and Yolanda Torres.

For contributions to this second edition, special thanks go to Carol Brunson Day, J. Ronald Lally, Louise Derman-Sparks, Deborah Chen, Sarah Garrity, Janet Gonzales-Mena, Alison Wishard Guerra, Elita Amini Virmani, and Peter L. Mangione. For editorial assistance, appreciation is extended to Eva Gorman.

The California Department of Education gratefully acknowledges Sara Webb Schmitz for the use of photos that appear in this publication and Deborah Greenwald for her work in selecting the photos. Special thanks also go to the following programs: Associated Students Inc. Children's Center, California State University, Sacramento; Blue Skies for Children; the Cameron School; Contra Costa Community College Early Learning Center; Eben Ezer Family Child Care; Little Munchkins Academy; Marin Head Start, Hamilton Campus; Marin Head Start, Indian Valley Campus; Marin Head Start, Meadow Park Campus; and Willow Street Schoolhouse.

About the Authors

Carol Brunson Day, PhD, is a native of Chicago. She holds a BA in psychology from the University of Wisconsin, an MA in early childhood education from the Erikson Institute, and a PhD in education from Claremont Graduate School.

Throughout her career in early childhood education, Dr. Day has been involved in both teaching young children and training teachers, at first as a Head Start teacher and instructor of child development at Prairie State College in Illinois. For 13 years, she was a member of the human development faculty at Pacific Oaks College in Pasadena, California, specializing in early childhood education and cultural influences on development. From 2005 to 2010, Dr. Day was the president of the National Black Child Development Institute after serving as the CEO and president of the Council for Professional Recognition from 1985 until 2004.

Dr. Day received two fellowship awards: the first in 1980 from the Ford Foundation and the National Research Council, and the second in 1981 when she was named a Shaughnessy Scholar under a program by the U. S. Department of Education's Fund for the Improvement of Post-Secondary Education

Louise Derman-Sparks, MA, has worked for more than 50 years on issues of diversity and social justice as a preschool teacher, child care center director, parent, college teacher, researcher, and activist. A native of New York City, she holds a BA degree with a major in English and a minor in history from Brooklyn College and an MA in early and elementary education from the University of Michigan. On the human development faculty of Pacific Oaks College, Pasadena, for 33 years, she is now a professor emeritus. Louise began her career as an early childhood educator in the Perry Preschool Project and the Ypsilanti Early Childhood Project and then directed a child care center in Los Angeles. She is the author and co-author of several books, the most recent work being *Anti-Bias Education for Young Children & Ourselves,* co-authored with Julie Olsen Edwards (2010). Other books include *What If All the Kids Are White?, Anti-bias/Multicultural Education with Young Children and Families* with Dr. Patricia Ramsey (2010), *Teaching/Learning Anti-Racism: A Developmental Approach* with Dr. Carol B. Phillips (1997), and *Anti-Bias Curriculum: Tools for Empowering Young Children,* with the A.B.C. Task Force (1989).

Ms. Derman-Sparks speaks, conducts workshops, and consults widely throughout the United States and internationally. A former member of the governing board of the National Association for the Education of Young Children, she currently works with Crossroads, an anti-racism training organization, and has been a social justice activist for 50 years. Ms. Derman-Sparks is also the mother of two children, Douglass and Holly Sparks, who are professionals in human services.

Deborah Chen, PhD, is a professor in the Department of Special Education at California State University, Northridge. Dr. Chen coordinates the Early Childhood Special Education credential program and teaches courses in this area. She has been an early interventionist; special educator; and administrator of programs for children with a variety of learning needs, severe and multiple disabilities, and sensory impairments. Dr. Chen's research, publications, and materials focus on the following areas: interdisciplinary perspectives in early intervention; communication with infants and young children who have multiple disabilities, visual impairments, and who are deaf-blind; and culturally responsive services to young children and families of diverse cultural and linguistic backgrounds. She has presented at statewide, national, and international conferences and has conducted professional development courses and workshops throughout the United States and internationally.

Alison Wishard Guerra, PhD, is an assistant professor in the department of education studies at the University of California, San Diego (UCSD). She received her PhD in education from the University of California, Los Angeles, in 2005, with an emphasis on psychological studies in education. Dr. Wishard Guerra's research focuses on culture and development in early childhood, with a particular focus on social and language development among Latino children from low-income families. Her research looks specifically at how social relationships and interactions may serve as protective factors for later cognitive development among at-risk children. She studies within-group variations related to immigration and acculturation experiences and their associations with children's developmental outcomes. Dr. Wishard Guerra is a member of the National Early Head Start Research Consortium, where she continues research investigating social and cognitive developmental outcomes. Within the consortium she leads a team to investigate the links betweenstability and continuity in early child care experiences and developmental outcomes of 3,000 children, from birth to three years old, participating in the Early Head Start National Research Project.

Dr. Wishard Guerra was a member of the expanded research consortia that developed the California Preschool Learning Foundations on English-language development, and she has served as an expert reviewer of English-language development and cultural diversity in the development of volumes 2 (Visual and Performing Arts, Physical Development, and Health) and 3 (History–Social Science and Science) of the *California Preschool Learning Foundations* and the *California Preschool Curriculum Framework,* published by the California Department of Education. Her current research at UCSD investigates the role of social pretend play in the development of oral language and school readiness among Mexican-heritage children. In the education studies department, she teaches courses on early childhood education; culture and developmental theory; quantitative research methodology; a dissertation-writing seminar; and research on curriculum design. Dr. Wishard Guerra is a 2009–10 Hellman Foundation Fellow and the recipient of a 2009–10 and 2011–12 University–Community (UC) Links grants. UC Links is a network of educational programs that connect community and university partners working together to create innovative after-school programs.

Sarah Garrity, EdD, received an MS in child and family development from San Diego State University and an EdD in educational leadership through a joint doctoral program offered by the University of California, San Diego, and California State University, San Marcos. She has been a practitioner in the field of early childhood education for almost 20 years as a teacher, administrator, and literacy coach. In her role as a Head Start administrator, she was responsible for implementation of Early Head Start and state-funded infant/toddler programs. Currently, she is an assistant professor in the Department of Child and Family Development at San Diego State University, where she teaches courses in early childhood education and for the department's early childhood mental health certificate program. Dr. Garrity's research focuses on using mixed methods and research techniques to learn more about the complexities of educational settings, particularly the cultural and linguistic origins of teacher practices and how they impact children's experiences and outcomes. Her research is committed to improving outcomes for at-risk children and closing the school-readiness gap through the use of classroom practices that are based on evidence and are meaningful and culturally relevant to both teachers and students.

Janet Gonzalez-Mena, MA, retired from working as a full-time faculty member in the child and family studies program at Napa Valley College and now is a self-employed consultant specializing in infants and toddlers, diversity, and partnerships with families. She was formerly director of child care services for a family service agency in San Mateo County. The agency's services included an infant/toddler center, a network of family child care homes, and a program of therapeutic child care for abused and neglected infants, toddlers, and preschoolers. She worked in Head Start as a teacher (when it first began) and later as a Head Start trainer. Her career includes being a home visitor in a bilingual program for Spanish-speaking children and their families. Ms. Gonzalez-Mena is the co-author of *Infants, Toddlers, and Caregivers: A Curriculum of Respectful, Responsive Care and Education* and the author of *Infant/Toddler Caregiving: A Guide to Routines.* She also wrote *Diversity in Early Care and Education: Honoring Differences.* She has written many articles about infants and toddlers, diversity, and parenting for periodicals, including *Young Children* and *Exchange Magazine.* She has a multiethnic, multiracial family.

Gisela Jia, PhD, is currently an associate professor in the department of psychology at Lehman College, City University of New York. She received her BA in English language and literature and her MA in linguistics from Beijing University and her doctorate in developmental and cognitive psychology from New York University. Throughout the past 17 years, she has conducted research in bilingual language development among first- and second-generation immigrants speaking Mandarin, Cantonese, Korean, Russian, or Spanish as their home language. Her work has been published in many professional journals, books, and proceedings read by psychologists, linguists, educators, and speech/language pathologists. Dr. Jia has involved many graduate and undergraduate students, as well as high school students, with multicultural and multilingual backgrounds in her research. She has served as a consultant for the California Department of Education to develop language learning standards for bilingual children.

Introduction

As early education programs strive to promote development for all children, those from diverse cultures as well as those from the mainstream, meeting the challenge of making everyone's culture visible will do more than merely improve program practice—it will reshape the entire field. To discover ways to educate all children, we must also consider the unique differences of individuals. An important influence on these differences is one's culture. As our understanding of culture's influence on the development of all people deepens, our understanding of human universals will increase. So as we work to discover the developing cultural child, we at the same time unveil the human child.

—Carol Brunson Day, *Concepts for Care: 20 Essays on Infant/Toddler Development and Learning*

Gilbert, Goode, and Dunne (2007) state that "Culture is the learned and shared knowledge that specific groups use to generate their behavior and interpret their experience of the world. It comprises beliefs about reality, how people should interact with each other, what they 'know' about the world, and how they should respond to the social and material environments in which they find themselves." Through culture, children gain a sense of identity, a feeling of belonging, and beliefs about what is important in life, what is right and wrong, and how to care for themselves and others. When children are raised only in their home culture, they learn those lessons almost effortlessly. But when they spend some of their formative years in child care with people who were not raised in their culture and who do not necessarily share the same family and community values, the learning of those important early lessons becomes more complex. That is the condition that many young children are now experiencing in the United States, as cultural diversity in child care is becoming the norm.

Because child care is becoming more culturally heterogeneous, infant/toddler care teachers can no longer be expected "naturally" to provide care that is consistent with parental care. Child care programs are experiencing an unparalleled growth in linguistic and cultural representation among the families and children served; therefore, understanding the impact of the out-of-home child care experience and the child's home culture on a child's development is crucial. The Program for Infant/Toddler Care is particularly concerned about the impact of the situation on children under three years of age. Research and practice have shown that for infants and toddlers to prosper in child care, their experiences should reflect a care teacher's sensitivity to the home culture. When out-of-home caregivers support the child's primary language and culture, they not only help the child develop, but also open the child care program's doors to the child's parents and community. Early caregiving in a child's native language and within familiar cultural rules makes child care a secure and supportive experience for the child. Culturally responsive care influences positively the development of identity, social competence, language, and intellectual competence.

This guide is written to assist infant/toddler care teachers in becoming more culturally responsive. It is intended to help teachers (1) better understand themselves and how they are influenced by their own cultural beliefs, (2) better understand the children and families they serve, and (3) learn a process for relating to cultural issues in a way that will help them become more effective teachers. The entire guide is based on three unifying themes that recur throughout the text:

- Cultural diversity is good and enriching for everyone.
- Cultural responsiveness is an ongoing process that continues to develop over time.
- Support of a child's full participation in his or her home culture is vital to optimal development.

The guide is divided into four sections, including a suggested resources section. Seven chapters written by experts in infant/toddler development, multicultural education, and cultural sensitivity underscore the need for culturally responsive infant/toddler care. The contributing authors present information, strategies, and insights for teachers working with infants and toddlers from culturally and linguistically diverse communities. The authors share the belief that commonalities and differences are fundamental to all humanity and that cultural diversity brings a rich mosaic to life. The purpose of the guide is to help readers analyze their own culturally driven behaviors, expand their ability to accept children and adults as they are, and respond more appropriately to people from cultural backgrounds different from themselves.

The first chapter, "Culture and Identity Development: Getting Infants and Toddlers Off to a Great Start," by Carol Brunson Day, provides a brief overview of identity development in the early years, highlighting the important role of infant/toddler care teachers in supporting the development of young children's positive sense of self as cultural beings. The author identifies basic characteristics of culture and discusses culturally responsive and consistent practices that empower infants and toddlers in multicultural child care settings. The chapter closes with practical ways for teachers to connect the cultural experiences of families and children to children's experiences in care.

The second chapter, "Prejudice, Bias, and Inequity in the Lives of Infants and Toddlers," by Louise Derman-Sparks, introduces readers to the ways in which prejudice, bias, and social inequity enter the lives of infants and toddlers. The chapter challenges readers to think deeply about messages regarding "who matters or does not matter, and who matters more" in early care settings and how these often subtle messages affect infant/toddlers'

sense of competence and well-being. Thoughtful and critical examination of one's own beliefs and biases regarding families served in the programs is recommended as the first step toward providing culturally responsive care. Additionally, elements of the early care setting (e.g., vision/mission, organizational culture, milieu, staff makeup and relationships with one another) are considered as central to building culturally responsive early care and education programs.

In the third chapter, "Inclusion of Children with Special Needs in Diverse Early Care Settings," Deborah Chen provides insight into some of the diverse perspectives that families hold around disability. Readers are introduced to early intervention terminology, eligibility criteria, and interventions for infants/toddlers with special needs. In addition, ways to support participation and a sense of belonging in the early care setting are discussed.

The fourth chapter, "A Cultural Communities and Cultural Practices Approach to Understanding Infant and Toddler Care," by Alison Wishard Guerra and Sarah Garrity, introduces readers to a new way of thinking about culture and its impact on development. A cultural communities and cultural practices lens is discussed as a powerful way to understand variations within ethnic and linguistic groups as opposed to making comparisons across these groups. Teachers can utilize this framework to explore with families how one's goals and values influence daily caregiving practices and routines.

The fifth chapter, "Cultural Sensitivity in Caregiving Routines: The Essential Activities of Daily Living," by Janet Gonzalez-Mena, examines the importance of ongoing and open communication between parents and child care providers. The author focuses on the caregiving routines of feeding, diapering and toileting, and sleeping and napping as examples of how established practices may conflict with the culturally based approaches of parents. An open attitude of respect is recommended in communicating with parents about routines in the child care program. Through an understanding of the cultural reasons behind caregiving practices and preferences, teachers may find acceptable ways to accommodate parents' requests.

The sixth chapter, written by Louise Derman-Sparks, takes the reader on an adventure of self-evaluation, challenge, and professional cultural growth. This chapter is relevant to the field of cultural awareness and sensitivity. Although it is not necessary to know everything there is to know about the cultures of the children with whom infant/toddler teachers work, the process of acknowledge, ask, and adapt challenges even the most experienced teacher to grow in cultural understanding. Through a process of thinking, writing, and evaluating, the reader learns concrete methods by which to identify, communicate, negotiate, and resolve issues of responsive caregiving.

The seventh chapter, "Creating Collaborative, Reciprocal Relationships with Linguistically Diverse Families," by Gisela Jia and Alison Wishard Guerra, discusses the complexities of working with young children from a wide array of linguistic and cultural backgrounds in early care settings. For young children, culture and language are essential to their developing sense of self and belonging. As such, continuity between the home and the care setting is recommended. This chapter offers a wide variety of strategies for teachers to engage with families in ways that support children's dual-language development and promote infant/toddlers' sense of belonging in early care settings.

References

Brunson Day, C. 2006. "Every Child Is a Cultural Being." In *Concepts for Care: 20 Essays on Infant/Toddler Development and Learning,* edited by R. Lally, P. Mangione, and D. Greenwald. San Francisco: WestEd.

Gilbert, J., T. D. Goode, and C. Dunne. 2007. "Cultural Awareness." From the *Curricula Enhancement Module* series. Washington, DC: National Center for Cultural Competence, Georgetown University Child Development Center.

Section One
Understanding the Social
Context of Infant/Toddler Care

Culture and Identity Development: Getting Infants and Toddlers Off to a Great Start

Carol Brunson Day

The Beginnings of Identity Development Are in Infancy

In crafting the preparation and training of infant and toddler care teachers, J. Ronald Lally calls for a focus on identity development as a central concern of infancy. He asserts:

> [I]n the process of forming [their] preliminary sense of self . . . part of what infants and toddlers get from caregivers are perceptions of how people act at various times and in various situations (seen as how the infant should behave), how people act toward them and others (seen as how they and others should be treated), and how emotions are expressed (seen as how they should feel). The infant uses these impressions and often incorporates them into the self she becomes. . . . More is happening than tender loving care and learning games—values and beliefs are being witnessed and incorporated. (Lally 1995, 58–59)

*T*he idea that an infant is not yet an individual (psychologically speaking)—but is in the process of becoming one—is widely accepted among experts in infant/toddler development. Although many factors influence this process, it is within the context of close, nurturing relationships that infants begin to see themselves as they are seen by others who are significant in their lives. In this context, infants begin to develop an identity, which is a set of organized beliefs about themselves that influences how they behave in social settings.

Right from the beginning of life, infants are competent in engaging in social interaction and very soon become sophisticated in their understanding of the social world. During their first year of life, infants begin to notice differences and similarities among people around them, including differences in skin color (Derman-Sparks and Olsen Edwards 2010; Katz and Kofkin 1997). Children as young as two years of age may begin to talk about the differences they see between people and begin to comment on these differences. Between the ages of three and five years, children may begin to include racial categories in how they identify themselves and others (Winkler 2009). When the caregivers in an infant's life are aware of the sophisticated ways in which children process information in their world, they can respond in a culturally responsive and sensitive manner. This is important because the way that teachers respond to infants and toddlers as the children notice differences between others and themselves influences how infants process these experiences and contributes to their developing sense of self.

As the number of child care and early education programs serving infants and toddlers increase, greater attention is focused on teachers' capacities to recognize that their actions are being perceived and interpreted by young children and incorporated into their definition of self that they are forming.

For example, Zero to Three has established this premise in its advice to parents, caregivers, and policymakers, arguing that "the development of strong attachment relationships with family and primary caregivers is a central task of infancy."[1] It is in the context of warm, loving relationships that infants learn to trust, to feel safe exploring their world, and to develop a sense of competence and confidence in their ability to master new skills. This growing sense of self-esteem and personal identity is a foundation for later success (Zero to Three 2009).

Dimensions of Identity Development

As this personal identity forms, children are also developing a reference group identity. In fact, Bordere and Morrison (2001) argue that children's developing sense of reference group identity stems from certain social contexts, including gender, class, ethnic, or racial group membership. Others have argued that maintaining an ethnic identity is particularly relevant when one's ethnic group is a "minority" group in the society

(Rosenthal 1987). Margaret Spenser and her colleagues (Swanson et al. 2009) maintain that, because personal identity and reference group orientation are inextricably bound together, understanding one's personal self as distinct from one's social group requires advanced cognitive abilities that neither infants/toddlers nor preschoolers possess developmentally. Nonetheless, as mentioned above, it is known that the sophisticated ways in which very young children process information allow them to notice skin-color differences and make group distinctions among people. Yet because personal identity and reference group identity, for infants, are interwoven, the messages they receive about the social group they can distinguish and identify with also has implications for their developing personal sense of self. Therefore, how these complex and highly significant parts of a child's self-identity are treated is important even in infancy.

Since culture shapes the context for the social interactions that form the fundamental building blocks of the various dimensions of identity, it is through cultural learning that children gain a feeling of belonging, a sense of personal history, and security in knowing who they are and where they come from. Although infants and toddlers are not capable of understanding abstract ideas about ancestry or how their family's culture fits into the larger society, Bodere and Morrison (2001) assert that it is never too early to demonstrate respect for children's cultural traditions. The fundamental question for infant/toddler identity becomes this: How do families and caregivers help infants and toddlers develop an identity that keeps them rooted in their culture and firmly attached to their family?

Zero to Three makes a solid case that goals for infants and toddlers' early learning must be developed with attention to issues of culture, ethnicity, and language in order for them to be accepted by members of different groups. This strategy is important because culturally authentic and consistent practice will contribute to the child's developing sense of self.

Culture, ethnicity, and language are incorporated by young infants into their sense of self through their relationships and experiences in their environment. "Each child learns how I am to behave and how others should be with me through culturally prescribed interactions" (Petersen et al. 2008, 21). Accordingly,

the child care environment should "be in harmony with what goes on at home, following the form and style of what is familiar to the child" (Lally n.d.).

The Role of Culture in Development

Although the early childhood field has a long history of commitment to developing culturally appropriate approaches to educating young children ("multicultural education"), it still struggles with understanding the role of culture in the development of our youngest children (Maschinot 2008; Derman-Sparks and Olsen Edwards 2010). To develop a culturally responsive approach, it is essential to understand that what children learn from parents and infant care teachers is an idea system that extends deep into the values of a group of people. Learning goes far beyond the things generally associated with culture, such as art, music, or styles of dress. As a child acquires cultural ways of being, these cultural rules for behavior impact identity by giving children the tools to understand their family/community and be understood in it. Acquiring the idea system of the group is so powerful that it gives children the ability to interact with the group. For example, babies are born with the capability to make sounds; however, those sounds become meaningful only as they communicate with their families. Through communication the sounds are shaped and organized into the words and sentences the babies' families use to share meaning. Thus, as children come to know the ideas that govern speech and language in their community, they gain the power to communicate and to represent themselves in the world.

So when infant/toddler care teachers treat culture with an almost exclusive emphasis on the celebrations, styles of dress, art, music, and food habits, they fail to appreciate the depth of cultural impact and the idea system at work in the process of development. Although a child's identity is impacted by participation in family cultural rituals, the focus neither starts nor ends there. Surrounding children with artifacts and customs that are a part of their history, homes, and communities is important. However, when that approach becomes the sole emphasis in attempts to embrace culture, it diverts attention from the more fundamental role that culture plays in the development of children's social, emotional, physical, and intellectual well-being. The challenge for infant care teachers and trainers of infant and toddler care teachers is to understand the importance of culture to human development and to move beyond mere cultural appreciation and enrichment to cultural empowerment.

Cultural Empowerment: Preparing Infant/Toddler Care Teachers for Competent Practice

This view about the ways that culture empowers the process of development is gaining ground in the field of early childhood education and care. Whereas the field once sought to teach children to appreciate the culture of others, or to enrich children's understanding of their own, now it strives to teach children in a culturally consistent context. Teachers must become aware that they probably will never learn a cultural curriculum that they will teach; instead, they will learn ways to relate to issues of culture. It will take work and study to understand the subtleties of how culture influences and empowers people. Such an endeavor is especially important for teachers responsible for the care of children who come from cultures that are different from the teachers.

The cultural empowerment approach helps the infant/toddler care teacher provide culturally consistent settings for children—settings built on the attitudes, values, and behavioral expectations of the home culture of the child. The knowledge that teachers need to create such settings resides in understanding the deep structure of culture and the way it works to support development.

Children build their basic sense of trust, security, and stability on cultural foundations learned at home. Therefore, continuity, consistency, and respect in the early care environment for cultural foundations are essential to children's growth. As stated in chapter 2, program practices vary in terms of continuity or discontinuity with the family's culture. When the family's culture is ignored or when infant care teachers react to children who are culturally different from them as though they are deficient, underdeveloped, or incompetent, children experience problems in communication, in getting their needs met, and in establishing relationships. Under those conditions, children lose the power to develop their overall well-being.

The cultural empowerment of children involves recognizing negative reactions to cultural differences and taking steps toward shifting these thoughts and reactions toward more affirmative ones. One way for infant/toddler care teachers to do this is to learn more about how culture is and is not transmitted. The following concepts are essential to helping teachers move toward a deeper understanding of cultural differences:

- Culture is a set of rules for behavior.
- Culture is characteristic of groups.
- Culture is learned.
- Individuals are embedded, to different degrees, within a culture.
- Cultures borrow and share rules.
- Members of a cultural group may be proficient in cultural behavior but unable to describe the rules.

Understanding these concepts will help in building relationships with families, a necessary part of providing culturally consistent and empowering care that supports identity development for infants and toddlers.

Culture as a Process

The six concepts mentioned above focus on the "deep structure of culture." They help promote an understanding of culture as a process. A more detailed discussion of each concept follows.

1. **Culture is a set of rules for behavior.** Culture cannot be "seen" because the rules are invisible; one can see only the products of culture: the behaviors produced by the rules. Nevertheless, cultural rules do not *cause* behavior; they *influence* people to behave similarly, in ways that help them to understand each other. It is by understanding a culture's rules that one knows how to greet a person younger than oneself, older than oneself, a friend, or a stranger. Cultural rules help teachers to know how to hold a baby. Cultural rules shape food preferences and celebrations—determine whether the sun or the moon is celebrated; whether to wear a dress or pants, or nothing at all. These rules give meaning to all the events and experiences of life. The essence of culture is not these behaviors themselves, but the rules that produce the behaviors.

2. **Culture is characteristic of groups.** The rules of a culture are shared by the group, not invented by the individual. The rules of the group, which are passed on from one generation to the next, form the core of the culture. It is a mistake to confuse individual differences with group cultural differences. Each person develops a unique personality as a result of his or her personal history and, at the same time, develops in a cultural context with some behavioral characteristics that are shared by other members of the group.

3. **Culture is learned.** No one is born acculturated; rather, each person is born with a biological capability to learn. What each person learns depends upon the cultural rules of the people who raised the person.

are conformists; others are nonconformists. Consequently, the behavior of members of cultural group will vary, depending on how deeply embedded their experiences are within the core of a culture. Thinking about behavioral variations in this way helps those who work with individual families to understand why, for instance, not all Japanese people "act Japanese."

Some rules are taught with words: "hold your fork in your right hand, and your knife in your left." Other rules are demonstrated by actions—when to smile, how close to stand when talking to someone, and so on.

Because culture is learned, it is a mistake to assume a person's culture by the way she or he looks. Someone may be racially black and culturally Irish. A person can also become bicultural or tricultural by learning the rules of cultures other than his or her own primary group.

4. **Individuals are embedded, to different degrees, within a culture.** Because culture is learned, it may be learned well by some people in the group and less well by others. As children are acculturated, they usually learn the core rules of their culture, yet they may not always learn each cultural rule equally well. Some families are more bound to tradition, others less so. Further, even though families and individuals learn the cultural rules, they may not always behave according to what have learned—some people

5. **Cultural groups borrow and share rules.** Each cultural group has its own set of core behavioral rules and is therefore unique; yet some of the rules of Culture A may be the same as the rules of Culture B. This happens because cultural rules evolve and change over time, and sometimes when two groups have extensive contact with one another, they influence each other in some areas. Thus two groups of people may speak the same language, yet have different rules about roles for women. Understanding of this concept helps to avoid confusion when a person from another culture is so much like the teacher in some ways, yet so different in other ways.

6. **Members of a cultural group may be proficient at cultural behavior but unable to describe the rules.** Acculturation is a natural process; as people become acculturated, they are not conscious that their ideas and behavior are being shaped by a unique set of rules. Just as a four-year-old who is proficient with language cannot diagram a sentence or explain the rules of grammar if

asked to do so, so also people may become thoroughly proficient with cultural behavior without consciously knowing that they behave according to rules. In the same way, understanding acculturation explains why one cannot walk up to a person and ask him or her to teach the culture. Teachers probably cannot explain theirs.

Culturally Responsive Practices That Support Identity Development

The following practices are culturally responsive and support identity development in infants and toddlers.

1. **Make a commitment to learn about the cultural expectations of the families whose children are in your care and eliminate any stereotyped and biased attitudes toward cultures different from your own.** There are no shortcuts to achieving this goal; it is a continuous process. A conscious choice is required to create a climate in which dialogue about culture occurs on a regular basis. In such a climate, infant care teachers and parents can raise issues openly, and decisions about what is best for children are collaborative, resulting from a negotiated consensus. Where to begin is not difficult—begin at the beginning. *Commit yourself to identifying and examining your own cultural biases with the aim of eventually eliminating them.* Remember that everyone has biases from growing up and living in a society in which negative attitudes and practices are institutionalized in the political, social, and economic systems that govern everyday life

(Katz 1978). Biases in institutional systems give privilege to one group over others by declaring the characteristics of that group superior to all others. Racist, classist, and sexist ideas must also be rejected. There are many written resources to help you explore your biases (see http://www.EdChange.org). Several organizations that specialize in such resources for educators are the Anti-Defamation League's A World of Difference Institute (http://www.adl.org/education) and Educational Equity Concepts (http://www.edequity.org).

2. **Actively search for subtle messages of bias in your daily life.** One beginning exercise to become aware of how biased messages subtly penetrate one's life involves examining the ways in which different people

and their behavior are represented on prime-time television. Arrange with a group of teachers, or with both teachers and parents, to watch a series of the same television programs; then meet for a follow-up discussion of what was seen and not seen on the television screen. You will probably find that the characters represent a limited range; in fact you might notice characters in roles that reflect typical stereotypes for their racial or cultural group; or you might notice the absence of members of diverse racial or cultural groups. No matter how much one may want to deny that those images affect one's attitude about various groups of people, they do. An important step in the exercise is to look for appropriate models in the community to counteract the negative mass-media stereotypes. This kind of exercise can help eliminate bias if it is carried out in a sensitive manner. Once bias is acknowledged, it is necessary to go beyond the negative images to the positive ones to be shared with the children in your care.

3. **Seek accurate information about the culture of the children in your care and determine how to use the information in the care setting.** Keep in mind the six concepts of acculturation presented earlier. Avoid focusing only on artifacts. Instead, try to get at the attitudes and values in the deep structure of the culture, knowing that various families are embedded to different degrees in their culture and that they may be unable to verbalize the cultural rules. Talk with families about what they do at home that

they feel is particularly culturally significant, what they consider to be the right and wrong ways to discipline children, and how they want their children to express anger or relate to authority figures. Ask how they feel children should act toward their friends and toward their siblings. Have them describe their style of bathing their babies, feeding them, and playing with them. Remember that you, too, operate on cultural rules and should share them in the discussions.

4. **Read about other cultures and discuss what you read with your families and colleagues.** Ask people from other cultures whether the information you read is of value and discuss with them when and how to apply it. A good deal of theoretical as well as practical material appears in the early childhood education literature. The Internet is an excellent way to locate resources (one example is the Web site http://www. EdChange.org). The most visible and well-known body of information in recent years has resulted from the multicultural education

movement that began in earnest in the 1960s (York 2006; Cross, Baker, and Stiles 1977). The movement has had an enormous impact and has generated a large body of curriculum material. Much of what has been written, however, contains stereotypes and biases. Be cautious and remain open to other people's opinions about what you read.

5. **Help families deal with issues of cultural conflict.** Children and families experience conflict when society devalues them by demanding that they give up their culture to achieve success (Delpit 1995; Hale 2001; Morris 1986). Often, families do not realize that young children can become bicultural. Family members think they must choose between their culture and the dominant one. Sometimes they feel that the dominant culture is more important, and they want their children to be successful in the broader society. That conflict can be resolved through open discussions and program approaches that support families in maintaining their cultural integrity while they are acquiring skills to function in the larger society.

6. **Work consciously to establish a program approach that helps chil-dren function in their own cultural community and builds their competence in the culture of the larger society.** Set up care settings that emphasize the following strategies:

   a. Use culturally appropriate (culturally empowering) child-rearing strategies in the daily functions of the care environment.

   b. Use children's home language to communicate with children and their families.

   c. Select and train program staff members who understand how culture influences their own behavior and who know the culture of the children.

   d. Establish agreed-upon strategies to foster development in the children's own culture. (For example, develop both English and the home language through the natural use of both languages in child care, whenever possible.)

   e. Establish agreed-upon strategies to facilitate the development in children of skills necessary for successful functioning in the dominant culture. (Development of such skills is most effectively done by programs with an additive approach, helping children to gain additional skills rather than substitute dominant-culture skills for home-culture skills.)

To grow and thrive, children need cultural skills—skills that will provide them with power and productivity in mainstream North America and with a sense of meaning in life, history, and home. With help, they will learn those skills and form views about who they are and who they can be. Children see themselves only as they are seen by the adults in their lives. When children see themselves through culturally responsive eyes, they will see their power.

References

Barrera, Isadora, Rob Corso, and Dianne McPherson. 2003. *Skilled Dialogue: Strategies for Responding to Cultural Diversity in Early Childhood.* Baltimore, MD: Paul Brookes.

Bordere, Tashel, and Johnetta Wade Morrison. 2001. "Supporting Biracial Children's Identity Development." *Childhood Education* 77 (3): 134–8.

Cross, Delores E., Gwendolyn C. Baker, and Lindley J. Stiles, eds. 1977. *Teaching in a Multicultural Society.* New York: Free Press.

Day, Carol Brunson. 2006. "Every Child Is a Cultural Being." In *Concepts of Care: 20 Essays on Child Learning and Development,* edited by J. Ronald Lally, Peter Mangione, Deborah Greenwald, 97–99. Sausalito, CA: WestEd.

Delpit, Lisa. 1995. *Other People's Children: Cultural Conflict in the Classroom.* New York: New Press.

Derman-Sparks, Louise, and Carol Brunson Phillips. 1997. *Teaching and Learning Anti-Racism: A Developmental Approach.* New York: Teachers College Press.

Derman-Sparks, Louise, and Julie Olsen Edwards. 2010. *Anti-Bias Education for Young Children and Ourselves.* Washington, DC: National Association for the Education of Young Children.

Derman-Sparks, Louise, and Patricia Ramsey. 2011. *What If All the Kids Are White? Anti-Bias Multicultural Education with Young Children and Families.* New York: Teachers College Press.

Gonzalez-Mena, Janet. 2001. "Cross-Cultural Infant Care and Issues of Equity and Social Justice." *Contemporary Issues in Early Childhood* 2 (3): 368–71.

Hale, Janice. 2001. *Learning While Black: Creating Cultural Excellence for African American Children.* Baltimore, MD: Johns Hopkins University Press.

Hale-Benson, Janice. 1986. *Black Children: Their Roots, Culture, and Learning Styles.* Baltimore: Johns Hopkins University Press.

Katz, Judith. 1978. *White Awareness: A Handbook for Anti-Racism Training.* Norman: University of Oklahoma Press.

Katz, P. A., and J. A. Kofkin. 1997. "Race, Gender, and Young Children." In *Developmental Perspectives on Risk and Pathology,* edited by S. Luthar, J. Burack, D. Cicchetti, and J. Weisz, 51–74. New York: Cambridge University Press.

Kendall, Frances E. 1983. *Diversity in the Classroom: A Multicultural Approach to the Education of Young Children.* New York: Teachers College Press.

Lally, J. Ronald. 1995. "The Impact of Child Care Policies and Practices on Infant/Toddler Identity Formation." *Young Children* 51 (1): 58–67.

———. n.d. Caring for Infants and Toddlers in Groups: Necessary Considerations for Emotional, Social, and Cognitive Development. [Handout from Module II, Introduction to Module II: Group Care training session]. Unpublished document. Sausalito, CA: The Program for Infant/Toddler Care.

Maschinot, Beth. 2008. *The Changing Face of the United States: The Influence of Culture on Child Development.* Washington, DC: Zero to Three.

Morris, Lee, ed. 1986. *Extracting Learning Styles from Social/Cultural Diversity: Studies of Five American Minorities.* Norman, OK: Southwest Teacher Corps Network.

Neugebauer, Bonnie, ed. 1992. *Alike and Different: Exploring Our Humanity with Young Children.* Rev. ed. Washington, DC: National Association for the Education of Young Children.

Petersen, Sandra, Lynn Jones, and Karen A. McGinley. 2008. *Early Learning Guidelines for Infants and Toddlers: Recommendations for States.* Washington, DC: Zero to Three.

Rosenthal, D. 1987. "Ethnic Identity Development in Adolescents." In *Children's Ethnic Socialization: Pluralism and Development,* edited by J. S. Phinney and M. J. Rotheram, 153–79. Newbury Park, CA: Sage Publications.

Swanson, Dena Phillips, Michael Cunningham, Joseph Youngblood, II, and Margaret Beale Spenser. 2009. "Racial Identity Development During Childhood." In *Handbook of African American Psychology,* edited by Helen A. Neville, Brendesha M. Tynes, and Shawn O. Utsey, 269–81. Thousand Oaks, CA: Sage Publications.

Winkler, Erin N. 2009. "Children Are Not Colorblind: How Young Children Learn Race." *Practical Approaches for Continuing Education* 3 (3): 1–8.

York, Stacy. 2006. *Roots and Wings: Affirming Culture in Early Childhood Programs.* St. Paul, MN: Redleaf Press.

Zero to Three. 2009. *Early Experiences Matter: A Guide to Improved Policies for Infants and Toddlers.* Washington, DC: Zero to Three. http://main. zerotothree.org/site/DocServer/Policy_ Guide.pdf?docID=8401 (accessed March 20, 2013).

CHAPTER 2

Prejudice, Bias, and Inequity in the Lives of Infants and Toddlers

Louise Derman-Sparks

The [United Nations Convention on the Rights of the Child] applies to all children, whatever their race, religion or abilities; whatever they think or say, whatever type of family they come from. It doesn't matter where children live, what language they speak, what their parents do, whether they are boys or girls, what their culture is, whether they have a disability or whether they are rich or poor. No child should be treated unfairly on any basis. (UNICEF 1990, 1)

Readers may wonder why this guide includes a chapter about prejudice, bias, and inequity and their relationship to the care and development of infants and toddlers. On the surface, the need to bring up racism, classism, or sexism would seem to be incongruous in the same breath as talking about child care for infants and toddlers. Yet, sadly, it is necessary. **Prejudice, bias,** and **societal inequity*** enter the lives of infants and toddlers in a variety of ways. Whether based on race, culture, gender, economic class, or family structure, these attitudes and realities have a negative, hurtful effect on the quality of life and development.

Although the child's immediate and extended family provides the primary environment of socialization in the infant/toddler years, much bias, prejudice, and societal inequity come from outside of the family. The professionals who provide infants and toddlers and their families with a range of services (e.g., child care providers, medical staff, social workers) are one source of the messages that convey whose way of life matters more and whose matters less. Some of these messages are obvious, some are subtle, and ironically, many are unintended. Some negative messages come from the attitudes and behaviors of the professionals. Many come from structural dynamics of the organizations in which human service professionals, including infant/toddler care teachers, work. These negative messages may include unexamined policies, procedures, and beliefs that create advantages for some groups and disadvantages for other groups.

The cumulative effect of messages about who matters (more or less) gradually influences how children begin

---

*Terms in boldface in this chapter are defined in the glossary on page 23.

to understand and feel about themselves and others—even in the first year of life. The messages also impact their quality of life. An understanding of the various forms of bias, prejudice, and inequity and how they influence infants and toddlers is critical to counteract potential damage to healthy development. Understanding grows from awareness, the first step to practicing culturally responsive, non-biased infant/toddler care that nurtures all children and families.

Societal Inequity and Families

Poverty is the social inequity that is most detrimental to infants and toddlers. In numerous ways, poverty denies families the resources they need to support optimal development. Housing may be available only in old, deteriorating buildings, which may be inadequately heated and ventilated, be overcrowded, and have toxic lead in the paint. Families living in

poverty are much more unlikely to afford health insurance. This means inadequate or no prenatal care and then insufficient well-baby care, since poor families often depend on hospital emergency care, sometimes travel long distances from home, and see less-experienced doctors after waiting for hours in crowded food is often of inferior quality and more expensive. No matter how loving and skilled the family is, the reality of poverty creates sometimes insurmountable barriers to optimum child-rearing.

Other factors may interact with poverty to add to these challenges. In the current political climate facing immigrants–especially undocumented immigrants—families may have no access to social services and health institutions that help support the family's quality of life. Families of all backgrounds, headed by a single mother, are more likely to live in poverty than are all other kinds of families. Poverty in rural areas is also an increasing reality, regardless of racial or ethnic background.

Although child care providers of infants and toddlers cannot change the conditions of families in poverty, gaining an understanding of the challenges created by poverty makes it possible to take action to mitigate its negative effects.

What Infants and Toddlers See and Hear in Child Care Settings

Messages about who matters or does not matter—and who matters more—are significant pathways of bias and inequality. The visual and auditory environment of an infant/toddler care and education program communicates many of these kinds of messages. These matter because infants and toddlers are just beginning to amass and process information about

themselves and others. And this awareness starts very early. For example, as
young as six months, infants begin to
notice differences in skin color (Bronson
and Merryman 2009; Katz 1976). Notic-
ing, paying attention to, or being curious
about differences and similarities in their
environment is not a sign of emerging
prejudice, but rather a characteristic of
how all children learn.

Inaccurate and stereotypical images
of people like themselves are one type
of bias that infants and toddlers may
encounter in the early care program.
Those images communicate misinformation about their own **social identities,**
which damages their developing sense
of self and family. They need accurate,
authentic photographs, posters, and
pictures of themselves and their families.
To begin to develop positive attitudes
toward people different from themselves,
infants and toddlers also need accurate
images about people different from themselves. They do not need misinformation
from commercialized, stereotypical, or
cartoon-looking images of people.

Visibility (or the lack thereof) is
another powerful pathway of bias and
inequity. When children see images of

people who look like them,
they receive a positive message
for their self-concept. However, seeing only images
similar to them conveys a
second, negative message:
only people like you exist or
are important. Conversely,
young children who do not
see images of people similar
to them in the early care and
learning environment receive
the message that they do not
matter as much as the people
whose images and languages
are visible. Experiencing invisibility
in an infant/toddler care and education
program is especially damaging, since it
is one of the first societal institutions that
very young children encounter.

The numerical balance of images that
reflect diverse racial identities, families,
and cultural ways of life also conveys
messages about who matters and who
matters more. When the majority of the

images in an infant/toddler care program reflect the way of life defined by the **dominant group** in society as the "normal" or right way to live, the message conveyed is that the dominant group is the most important. When one cultural group's way of life becomes the standard for everyone else, the seeds of racial and cultural advantage and disadvantage are sown.

In addition to the visual environment, the sounds of a program also convey information about whose family's way of life matters or not. The language of the program is the most obvious source of sound—and it may or may not be what infants and toddlers hear at home. Hearing a language different from the one at home creates a more complicated adjustment and developmental challenge for infants and toddlers than that experienced by those whose home language matches the program's language. Similarly, the sounds of music and song evoke—or do not evoke—the security of home, depending on how similar or different they are from what an infant is used to.

A growing body of research also indicates that misinformation and prejudice about social identity harm children's development (e.g., Derman-Sparks and Ramsey 2004; Tatum 2003). The negative impact is cumulative—coming not just from overt "bigotry" or messages of direct prejudice, but also from the effect of small "micro-contaminants" in the way others interact with them as well as messages of invisibility regarding who they are (Pierce 1980). These messages and actions in their daily lives gradually build up to become toxic to children's sense of self, well-being, and competence. A nonbiased environment is a necessary condition for nurturing each child's healthy identity and positive attitudes about diversity. However, the visual and

auditory environment is only one component of culturally responsive programs.

Socialization in Two Cultures

The widespread use of outside-the-home group and family infant/toddler care signifies that, for the first time in human history, the family—nuclear and extended—is no longer the only primary child-rearing environment of infants and toddlers. This means that in the earliest years, hundreds of thousands of children experience two differing cultural contexts every day—that of the family and that of early care and education. Thus, cultural continuity in child-rearing is disrupted. Paying attention to cultural continuity and cultural discontinuity between home and infant/toddler care programs is the central issue in a culturally responsive approach.

Where an infant/toddler's experiences fall on the continuity-discontinuity continuum depends on the degree of similarity or difference between the specific cultural dynamics of their family and those of the early childhood program. These include fundamentals such as furniture, equipment, spatial organization, care procedures, language, and how staff members interact with the children and each other. Some infants and toddlers experience a high degree of continuity, while others experience a high degree of discontinuity. The more discontinuity infants and toddlers face, the more they find that what they are learning in their family about how to be in the world does not work for them in the care program.

The long-term effects on very young children's development when they experience discontinuity between their two primary socialization environments are not known. However, it is clear that the degree of familiarity or unfamiliarity with a program's care practices makes it easier or harder for infants and toddlers to adjust, to build strong relationships, to act and feel competent, and to feel secure. It is also known that a primary source of a child's sense of belonging, security, and empowerment in a child care and education program comes from as much continuity as possible with what

children experience in their home culture, as chapter 1 suggests. Young children thrive when an early childhood program respects and integrates their home languages and cultures into all of its operations. In such programs, children can learn and develop because they feel "supported, nurtured, and connected not only to their home communities and families but also to teachers and the educational setting" (NAEYC 1995, 2). In sum, when an infant/toddler's home culture (including language) differs significantly from the culture of her/his child care program, she does not have the opportunity to thrive.

Practicing Culturally Responsive Care

The goal of culturally responsive care and education is to create and foster an equal playing field for all the infants and toddlers in a program. This goal requires minimizing the discontinuity between each child's home and the infant/toddler program, as well as eliminating inaccurate, stereotypical, and inauthentic messages about all people. It also requires that early childhood education (ECE) professionals work to understand their own cultural beliefs and behaviors about the

raising of infants/toddlers, and thoughtfully, critically examine their beliefs, information, and biases regarding the families whom they serve. Thus, culturally responsive care also incorporates the goals of anti-bias education (Derman-Sparks and Olsen Edwards 2010).

Critical examination of the premises and culture

of the infant/toddler care and education field, which has its own set of values, rules, information, and acceptable behaviors, is another element of culturally responsive care and education. Many of the tenets that underlie the infant/toddler care culture are grounded in this country's dominant culture—Western, affluent, European-Anglo. These do not necessarily match what is considered "normal development" and "best practices" across all ethnic/cultural lines. Consequently, some beliefs and approaches of the ECE field may unintentionally become a source of bias and inequity when they create a high degree of cultural discontinuity for an infant or toddler.

However, culturally responsive care does not require teachers to abandon all that they have learned about infant/toddler development in order to create high-quality group care/learning environments, as some people fear. It does mean knowing how to learn from each family about what matters to them and learning how to engage in an ongoing blending of home and ECE culture. It also means knowing how to support the children and families who are being asked to make the greatest adjustments. The culturally responsive approach also does not mean integrating everything a family does into the program—this is not really possible, because the group of families the program serves practice their culture in their particular way. Even when all the families come from the same ethnic and cultural group, they most likely do not do everything in the same manner. However, as Carol Brunson Day points out, a program's customary way is not the only way:

> *We can learn principles for creating culturally consistent programs. However, there is no recipe for being there. The* there *is built by you with families and staff. It is always a dynamic process and depends on the people who are together in a program at any given time. It calls on everyone to be willing to negotiate and compromise if necessary. If you stay open to the fact that your way is not the only right way, trust in the ability of people to figure out differences, and really work on it, you can get to where you want your classroom to be. When everyone has access to deciding on a solution that works for them, then there is real equality.* (Derman-Sparks and Olsen Edwards 2010, 61)

As teachers learn about each child's home culture, they will find that some practices that come from their own cultural background and from their ECE training must be adapted or rethought for some children in order to create continuity with their families' cultures. The NAEYC (2009) recognizes this fact, specifying that for any practice to be developmentally appropriate it must take into account not only a child's age group and individual characteristics but also the social and cultural contexts in which the child lives. Thus, culturally responsive infant/toddler care environments do not look like a "universal or model" program; nor do they look exactly like any one family's home culture. Rather, a culturally responsive infant/toddler program continually evolves and changes as the composition of the program (children, families, and staff) changes and as the staff gets better at learning from families and making adaptations as needed

(Derman-Sparks and Olsen Edwards 2010, chapter 5). Making ongoing adaptations to connect with children and families is what this guide will help you learn to do.

Building Blocks of a Culturally Responsive Care/Learning Environment

This final section of the chapter takes an overall look at the elements that must be continually developed, implemented, and assessed to build a culturally responsive care/learning program. Chapters 4–7 then offer a range of specific strategies for putting these building blocks in place.

Vision/mission: A vision statement expresses what a program is working toward. It is an inspiration and guide as well as an expression of hope (Carter and Curtis 2010). The mission statement briefly sums up the framework in which a program operates. Both the vision and mission statements set the course for the daily practice of a program. A culturally responsive program explicitly spells out this value and concept.

Organizational culture: The culture of an organization—its leadership, structure, management systems, and relationships—

makes the program's vision come to life. Resources must be marshaled to make a culturally responsive approach concrete every day in all aspects of the program. Otherwise, a culturally responsive vision and mission stays only on paper. A culturally responsive program is committed to open, respectful conversations with each family and ongoing changes to create continuity between the family's home and the program.

Goals: Set specific goals at the beginning and revisit them throughout the program year. Goals must reflect the culturally responsive mission and a strategic plan for achieving it. For example, beginning-of-the-year goals might include developing an agreed-upon vision and mission, assessing the visual/aesthetic environment, engaging staff members in conversations about cultural backgrounds and their influence on work

with children, and planning how to build respectful relationships with families. Three months into the year, goals might include completing in-depth conversations with every family about child-rearing goals and practices and developing a comprehensive plan for how staff will systematically integrate family needs into the daily program. A midyear goal might be to assess what progress has been made in building a culturally responsive milieu and adapting program practices to reflect thinking about ECE best practices and families' needs. If a program has already achieved these kinds of goals, then the beginning-of-the-year goals might include assessing what they have achieved and setting goals for improvement in each area of the program. It might also include goals for deepening their critical thinking about ECE best practices.

Milieu: This category includes the program's visual/aesthetic appearance, all images in the environment, the sounds and language, equipment, and organization of space. A diversity-rich, stereotype-free visual and auditory environment provides the sights and sounds that young children need to develop positive self-awareness and comfortable relationships with others. The first rule of thumb is for all the children and families in the program to be respectfully and equitably reflected in the environment. A culturally responsive environment reflects the rich variety within cultural and ethnic groups, as well as the wider diversity in the U.S.A. Each staff member has the responsibility to ensure that no child and family are invisible and no stereotypical or insulting images of any group are present.

Assess everything in the visual/auditory environment. For example, in a toddler room, do all of the art materials include various shades of black and

brown? Are dolls—big and small—diverse? Does the collection of picture books equitably and accurately depict people who look like the children and families in the program and also introduce diversity among people beyond the program and equipment? Equipment also matters. For example, not all babies sleep in the same kind of furniture. Do the infants sleep at home in cribs, in hammocks, in cradles, in the same room with their parents or siblings, or alone in their own rooms? This information is valuable to know.

Be creative in solving cultural differences. Carol Brunson Day shares an example she observed in one infant/toddler program (Derman-Sparks and Olsen Edwards 2010): Licensing rules (and the NAEYC Accreditation Criteria) require children to nap in their own cribs. However, some of the babies served by the center sleep in hammocks at home, and they will not go to sleep in the cribs. So the staff became creative. Staff members tied hammocks diagonally from the crib posts, so that each infant slept in a position comfortable to them while still being in cribs.

Caregiving procedures and other interactions with infants/toddlers: This element of a culturally responsive infant/toddler program goes to the core of culture. Young children are not only continually absorbing information learning about themselves and others from the sights and sounds of the environment, they also learn about how to be in the world from the relationships they have with the people who care for them, the care routines (e.g., eating, sleeping, eliminating), and the interactions between adults and themselves when they hurt themselves, cry, are scared or happy. All of these interactions transmit important messages about whom an infant/toddler care and education program values and ways of being in the world.

In a culturally responsive care and education program, staff members critically assess the degree to which all staff–child interactions, including the basic care procedures, such as diaper changing, eating, sleeping, comforting, and the like, are continuous or discontinuous with the infant/toddlers' homes (for a more in-depth discussion of this topic, see chapter 5). They also consider the degree to which cultural discontinuous interac-

tions make it easier or harder for the infants/toddlers to develop comfortable, supportive relationships with their caregivers. Teachers are also willing and able to make changes in their practice as needed. Assessment and changes in practice are ongoing, as staff members learn from and collaboratively work with families. Sections Two and Three provide tools for implementing these essential, culturally responsive strategies.

Language continuity and discontinuity: This element is also central to socialization and the home–infant/toddler program cultural contexts in which language development takes place. As stated in chapter 1, infants and toddlers are beginning to learn the language of their family. However, for many infants and toddlers, their family's language differs from that of the larger society—and, usually, from the language spoken in the early childhood program. A culturally responsive environment tackles this challenging reality based on information about language development and not personal opinion or political ideology. The subject is so essential that it merits its own chapter, "Creating Collaborative, Reciprocal Relationships with Linguistically Diverse Families" (chapter 7).

Relationships with children's family and community: In a culturally responsive care-and-education program, families are indispensable partners. They are the primary source from whom staff members learn about the particular cultural dynamics in each infant/toddler's home. As the NAEYC advises all early childhood programs:

> *Practitioners work in collaborative partnerships with families, establishing and maintaining regular, frequent two-way communication with them . . . [They] involve families as a source of information about the child . . . and engage them in planning for their child. . . Mutual respect, cooperation, and shared responsibility inform these family-teacher relationships. (NAEYC 2009, 23)*

A chapter in this book is devoted to the topic of how to build collaborative, reciprocal relationships with linguistically diverse families.

Staff makeup and relationships with each other: All members of the staff (e.g., the director, teachers, teacher assistants, cook, custodian, and so forth) are part of the care and learning environment. Ideally, the staff is made up of people who come from backgrounds similar to the children and families served, with some diversity of racial identity, language and home culture. It is also essential to build relationships of respect and collaboration among all staff members, as well as a culture of providing support for each other's growth in becoming culturally responsive. As one of the NAEYC's position statements explains:

> *Because early childhood settings tend to be children's first communities outside the home, the character of these communities is very influential in development . . . The foundation for the community is consistent, positive, caring relationships . . . It is the responsibility of all members of the learning community to consider and contribute to one another's well-being and learning. (NAEYC 2009, 16)*

Conclusion

Ultimately, creating culturally responsive programs requires early childhood professionals to travel on a journey of awareness, learning, and change. Biased and inequitable behavior is not just what others do. Nor is it necessarily or always intentional. Every person who works with children and families should take this journey. This requires willingness to do the sometimes hard and uncomfortable work of uncovering biases, areas of misinformation, and insufficient information in one's thinking and in accepted beliefs about early childhood care and education. It also requires a critical examination of the daily activities that impact the infants, toddlers, and families served by a program.

Of course, culturally responsive care and education also brings challenges. It is a more complex approach than working from only one cultural perspective. It requires continual staff self-reflection, program assessment, learning, and adaptation of staff practices to diverse family socialization practices. Teachers face the realities of group care, where several different home cultures may be present and even families from the same cultural group likely live their culture in some different ways. Culturally responsive care also obliges teachers to be reflective practitioners, adapting their professional training and teaching to the diversity of the infants/toddlers and families in the program. In addition, teachers have to take into account licensing requirements and other regulations. All of this takes ongoing discussion and problem solving by staff. Ultimately, programs must do the best they can to implement the principles of culturally inclusive care and education, although it is often not possible to do it one hundred percent.

However, the work is worth it because everyone benefits from culturally inclusive care and education. The infants/toddlers being served are much more likely to thrive. Families will know that their precious children are safe, and it will be more likely that families will work productively with teachers. Staff also gains. Staff members are able to

grow more fully as human beings, with a better understanding of both themselves and others. Finally, early childhood practitioners are better able to meet the core professional goal of nurturing all children toward their fullest development.

In the foreword to a book about anti-bias education, Carol Brunson Day wrote something that is equally true for culturally responsive education: "[S]hould you choose to fully engage on the journey, your reward will be a renewed sense of hope that by your own hand, things really can change" (Derman-Sparks and Olsen Edwards 2010, vi).

Glossary*

bias. An attitude, belief, or feeling that results in and helps to justify unfair treatment of a person because of his or her identity.

dominant group. A group within a society that has the greatest power, privileges, and social status. It may or may not constitute the majority of the

---

*Definitions from Derman-Sparks and Olsen Edwards 2010.

population. Throughout much of the history of the United States, the dominant group has been white, Christian, affluent, and male.

prejudice. An attitude, opinion, or feeling formed without adequate prior knowledge, thought, or reason. Prejudice can be prejudgment for or against any person, group, or gender.

social identities. Membership in groups that are defined by society, are shared with many other people, and have societal advantages and disadvantages attached to them. These identities include gender, economic class, racial identity, heritage, religion, age group, and so on.

social inequity. The outcomes of laws, policies, procedures, and practices that place people at an advantage or disadvantage based on their social identity.

References

Bronson, P., and A. Merryman. 2009. "See Baby Discriminate." *Newsweek* (September 14): 53–59.

Carter, M., and D. Curtis. 2010. *The Visionary Director.* St. Paul, MN: Redleaf Press.

Derman-Sparks, L., and J. Olsen Edwards. 2010. *Anti-Bias Education for Young Children and Ourselves.* Washington, DC: National Association for the Education of Young Children.

Derman-Sparks, L., and P. Ramsey. 2011. *What If All the Kids Are White? Anti-Bias Education for Young Children and Families.* 2nd ed. New York: Teachers College Press.

Katz, P. A. 1976. "The Acquisition of Racial Attitudes in Children." In *Towards the Elimination of Racism,* edited by P. A. Katz, 125–154. New York: Pergamon.

National Association for the Education of Young Children (NAEYC). 1995. *Responding to Linguistic and Cultural Diversity: Recommendations for Effective Early Childhood Education.* Position statement. Washington, DC: NAEYC.

———. 2009. *Developmentally Appropriate Practice in Early Childhood Programs Serving Children from Birth through Age 8.* Position statement. Washington, DC: NAEYC.

Pierce, C. M. 1980. "Social Trace Contaminants: Subtle Indicators of Racism." In *Television and Social Behavior: Beyond Violence and Children,* edited by S. Withey, R. Abeles, and L. Erlbaum, 249–57. Hillsdale, NJ: Erlbaum.

Ramsey, P. G. 2004. *Teaching and Learning in a Diverse World.* 3rd ed. New York: Teachers College Press.

Tatum, B. D. 2003. *"Why Are All the Black Kids Sitting Together in the Cafeteria?" and Other Conversations about Race.* 2nd ed. New York: Basic Books.

UNICEF. 1990. "Fact Sheet: A Summary of the Rights under the Convention on the Rights of the Child." New York: UN General Assembly. http://www.unicef.org/crc/files/Rights_overview.pdf (accessed March 20, 2013).

CHAPTER 3

Inclusion of Children with Special Needs in Diverse Early Care Settings

Deborah Chen

Families that have very young children with special needs are almost always concerned about how their children will fare in early care and education settings—how they will be treated and what special accommodations will be made for them. With time, effort, and a welcoming climate in the early care setting, infant/toddler care teachers can develop relationships with families that help them trust that their concerns for their child will be addressed. Essential to the development of this trusting relationship is the pursuit, by infant care teachers, of information about each individual family—its values, beliefs, and child-rearing practices—so as to facilitate continuity between the child's experiences at home and in the early care setting.

Differences in cultural backgrounds, educational levels, and roles of teachers and family members may contribute to differing values, beliefs, child-rearing practices, and notions about how to relate to a child's special need, and, in turn, negatively impact attempts at maintaining continuity. The key to building continuity of care between home and early care settings for children is for teachers to respect differences they may have with families and to use a warm and welcoming style that conveys interest in and commitment to the family's perspective. This chapter explores a culturally responsive approach to including children with special needs in infant/toddler care. It shares some ideas about disability that families hold. It defines early intervention terminology and offers ways to gather information from families to support inclusion of infants and toddlers with special needs in early childhood settings. Finally, it recommends strategies for partnering with families of diverse linguistic and cultural backgrounds.

Diverse Perspectives on Disability

A family's understanding of their child's special need may be quite different from that of other families and from

that of teachers and early intervention service providers. For example, families from one cultural group may view the child's special need as a natural part of life or spiritual phenomenon that is to be accepted without outside intervention. Other families may believe that they have a God-given responsibility to do everything possible to care for their child. Still other families may believe that the child's special need is due to very bad luck or a misdeed committed by a member of the family or of the child in a former life (Lynch and Hanson 2011). These varied beliefs may influence child-rearing practices, expectations of the child, and the family's willingness to be involved in early intervention services. Similarly, professionals may have a specific clinical or medical view of the child's special need that may compel them to recommend interventions to promote the child's developmental skills and remediate difficulties in particular ways.

One common way of viewing the successful development of children in the United States is to see individuality or independence as a strength to be mastered early. In other countries, and in particular cultural communities in the U.S., a focus on group membership and interdependence is more common. Early intervention services in the United States often stress the infant's development of independence, particularly in the areas of daily living skills and motor development, but some families may not have these particular goals for their very young children. Such differences between professionals and families can be resolved only through a process of sharing perspectives, understanding each other's point of view, and reaching mutual agreements.

Each morning, Mr. Sanchez carries his daughter Anna into the toddler classroom, and when he picks her up a few hours later he carries her to the car. Sometimes Anna arrives drinking from a baby's bottle. She is almost three years old (34 months) and has Down syndrome. Two goals for her on her transition Individualized Family Service Plan (IFSP) are to walk without support and to drink from a cup. Anna has begun to walk without support in the classroom and to take a few sips from a cup at snack time. Ms. McKay, her teacher, wants Anna to be ready for preschool when she has her third birthday and is concerned about her delays in walking, self-feeding, and other areas of development. Rather than stereotyping the father's behavior as being "overprotective," she decides to learn more about the family's values and goals for Anna's development. In this way, she hopes to develop a shared understanding with the family about Anna's care. Ms. McKay decides on the following steps:

1. *Initiate a conversation with Mr. Sanchez about his goals, priorities, and expectations regarding Anna's development and when she begins preschool.*

2. *Find out about the father's perspective on Anna's walking by herself and why she likes to drink from the baby bottle.*

Mr. Sanchez indicates that he knows Anna should learn to walk on her own. However, he is concerned about (a) the time and energy this will take each day, (b) her safety, and (c) her tolerance for walking to and from the classroom. When they arrive in the morning, Anna fusses and wants to be picked up when he gets her out of her car seat. He gives Anna a bottle in the car because it comforts her during the transition from home to the center, she does not have time to finish her breakfast in the morning, and he does not want her to be hungry when she arrives. He believes that his responsibility is to keep Anna safe and happy rather than teach her to walk during the hectic drop-off and pickup times at the center. He admits feeling a little guilty about leaving her at this program with strangers even for a few hours, although he knows that Anna enjoys being there, but he needs to get to work. Once Ms. McKay has listened carefully to the father's comments, she acknowledges the benefits of giving Anna a bottle in the car. She also says that, when needed, Mr. Sanchez can bring the leftover breakfast to the center for Anna to finish eating it. Ms. McKay asks whether there are convenient times at home to help Anna drink from a cup. She also shares how Anna is encouraged and helped to drink from a cup in the center. Mr. Sanchez and Ms. McKay also agree that the father will carry Anna from the car to the door of the classroom and that Ms. McKay will encourage her to walk from the door to a favorite area in the room.

In this vignette, Ms. McKay demonstrates critical interpersonal and professional skills that facilitate development of collaborative relationships with families. She maintains a nonjudgmental, respectful, and open attitude in gathering information; clearly identifies and discusses the area of concern with Mr. Sanchez; listens to and accepts his point of view and recognizes its value; and then offers ways to address both of their concerns. In this way, she demonstrates interest in and commitment to supporting Anna's development and an appreciation of partnering with the family. Once the family's circumstance and perspectives are understood, the teacher is able to offer suggestions that are both aligned with the family's priorities and are in the best interest of the child.

Differences in Perspectives

Differences in beliefs, values, and caregiving practices may contribute to differences in opinions between families and early intervention service providers and teachers about how best to support a child's learning and development. For example, an early childhood program may not condone the use of walkers for toddlers, but a physical therapist may recommend a specialized walker for a 30-month-old with cerebral palsy. A speech and language therapist may suggest the use of signs for key words

for an 18-month-old with developmental delays, but the child's family is concerned that the use of manual signs will inhibit the child's speech development. In these situations, it is helpful for all parties involved to have a conversation about each person's perspective about the issue. The focus of these conversations should include (a) learning about the basis of each concern; (b) identifying a common goal for the child's development; (c) agreeing on which practice will be tried, the specified period of time for the practice, and who will be involved; and (d) scheduling a follow-up meeting.

Understanding Early Intervention Terminology, Eligibility, and Intervention

When an infant or toddler is identified as being eligible for early intervention services, the family will likely be introduced to an unfamiliar process with its own terminology. Teachers who understand a family's cultural perspective regarding the meaning of the child's disability and of the intervention process can help families make sense of this new terminology.

Early intervention is a system of services for young children (birth to 36 months) with special needs and their families. Part C of the Individuals with Disabilities Education Act (IDEA)—a federal law—mandates early intervention services (U.S. Department of Education 2011).

The purpose of early intervention is to provide supports to children and families that will promote early learning and development, but this purpose cannot be achieved without the collaborative efforts of the family and the early care and intervention services. Typically, early intervention services are provided in a variety of settings. Priority should be placed on providing services in a natural environment, one in which the child would function if he or she did not have a special need. For infants and toddlers, natural environments include the family home, child care, early childhood, and community settings with typically developing peers. Natural environments allow children to learn and develop skills in everyday activities and social interactions in the very environments in which the skills are used and needed. Because families may not be familiar with the importance of natural environments, it may be helpful for teachers to assist families in understanding why natural environments are preferred.

Eligibility for Early Intervention Services

To be eligible for early intervention services, the very young child (i.e., birth to 36 months of age) must be identified as having a developmental delay in one or more areas of development (cognitive, physical, communication, social/emotional, and or adaptive); or an established risk or diagnosed condition that has a high probability of resulting in a developmental delay (e.g., Down syndrome, cerebral palsy, autism, visual impairment, hearing loss, or multiple disabilities); or a biological or environmental risk such as medical (e.g., prematurity) or home conditions (e.g., parents with disabilities) that may significantly compromise a child's development if early intervention is not provided (U.S. Department of Education 2011).

The term *developmental delay* indicates that a young child is not demonstrating behaviors that are typical for his or her age. Some of these children will catch up with typically developing peers, whereas some of these children may always acquire skills at a slower rate, develop some skills but not others, or may never "catch up" developmentally. It is important for teachers and families to understand the meaning of the child's eligibility category in order to obtain needed services and resources. Teachers who establish respectful relationships with families can help them gain a shared understanding of the diagnosis and eligibility category.

Initiating the Early Intervention Process: Making Referrals

Given their knowledge about early childhood development and experience with infants and toddlers, teachers are likely to notice when a child does not meet expected developmental milestones or engages in atypical behaviors. Atypical behaviors may include, but are not limited to, a lack of interest in social interactions, excessive energy levels, difficulty changing from one activity to another, extreme sensitivities to different sounds or textures, or repetitive actions with objects (e.g., spins them). The intensity and persistence of such unusual behaviors may indicate the need for a referral for developmental

screening, particularly if the child cannot be guided to more developmentally appropriate interactions. Teachers should discuss their observations to determine whether the family has also noticed these behaviors at home and ask if they are concerned about them.

As discussed previously, families have a variety of caregiving practices and expectations about young children's development and behaviors. For example, some toddlers may not have opportunities to move around on the floor at home so the family may not have observed how the child crawls or walk. This lack of experience may contribute to what appears to be clumsiness when this child moves around the classroom. Another family may not be concerned if their little boy displays aggressive behaviors, as they believe that boys must be bold and forceful. Behaviors that teachers find worrisome may be quite acceptable to some families. It is therefore important for teachers to recognize the profound influence of family, home, and culture on a child's behavior and development and simultaneously be familiar with unusual behaviors or high-risk signs that may indicate the need to refer a child for developmental screening. Teachers should notice whether a child shows any of the following signs (Cook, Klein, and Chen 2012).

Behavioral Signs

- Avoids or rarely makes eye contact
- Does not seek comfort or approval from a familiar caregiver or parent
- Stares into space or sits and rocks body more often than children of the same age
- Shows more frustration, acting out, or aggressive behaviors compared with other children
- Gets easily upset (e.g., by changes in familiar routines or loud, sustained sounds such as a vacuum cleaner) and has great difficulty calming him or herself

Physical Signs

- Arms or legs are stiff
- Body posture is limp compared to other children of the same age
- Uses one side of the body more than other
- Seems physically clumsy compared with children of the same age

Vision Signs

- Has difficulty visually following objects or persons

- Turns or tilts head in an unusual position when looking at an object
- Has difficulty making eye contact
- Brings objects very close to eyes
- Has poor eye–hand coordination
- Eyes appear to turn in or out

Hearing Signs

- Does not startle when there are loud, sudden noises
- Does not develop sounds or words that are used by children of the same age and home language
- Does not respond to his or her name when called from across the room
- Makes sounds or talks in a very loud or soft voice
- Turns or cocks head to hear speaker

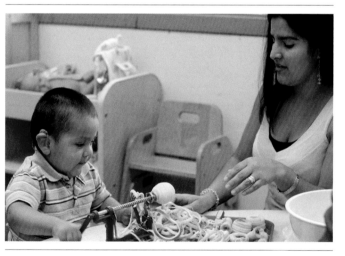

If a child exhibits any of these signs, record observations in writing during natural, everyday activities that call for the child to exhibit his or her abilities and behaviors. Note the child's skills and discuss them and any unusual behaviors with the family.

If parents have concerns about their child's development, teachers should explain the referral process for obtaining a developmental screening and ask for the parents' permission to initiate a referral. Teachers should also help parents understand the purpose of developmental screening, who conducts them, what is involved, and how the results may be used. The purpose of a developmental screening is to obtain information about a child's milestones and basic skills. A variety of trained professionals may be qualified to conduct developmental screenings, including, physicians, nurses, psychologists, and early childhood special education personnel. The screening process may include a variety of methods—for example, administration of a standardized assessment tool, observations, and interviews with significant caregivers. Information about the child's development is used to determine whether the child has a developmental delay that indicates the need for referral to early intervention services.

Teachers play an important role in helping families get access to and negotiate an unfamiliar early intervention service system. It is important that teachers take into account the family's culture, language, and beliefs when interpreting an infant/toddler's behavior. However, determining whether a behavior deserves attention by a professional or if it is just different from what a teacher expects to see may be difficult. Consider the following example:

Sixteen-month-old Jiyun Park has just joined Monica's infant group. Jiyun is a happy child who babbles a lot, although she has been identified as having a developmental delay. The family's home language is Korean; however, both parents speak English in the community. Monica asks Mrs. Park about the Korean words that Jiyun understands and says, as well as the meaning of the words. Monica learns that Korean parents use certain words with their very young children—such as "mam ma," which means food, and "kka kka," which means small snacks or crackers. Monica is very surprised to discover the true meaning of Jiyun's vocalizations, as she was misinterpreting them based on her own language background and experiences.

Monica's experience highlights that learning about the family's home language is essential to appreciating a child's language development and communication efforts. Through her conversation with Mrs. Park, Monica realizes that she mistakenly assumed that Jiyun's vocalizations were merely babbling sounds. Now she understands that Jiyun is actually using words intentionally to make requests. Monica shares this important information with the classroom staff so that everyone can interpret and respond appropriately to Jiyun's use of words.

In another classroom, 24-month-old Billy Patel has been in the toddler group for about three weeks. He wanders around the classroom and gets upset if an adult tries to guide his participation in activities with other children. His teacher, Evelyn, realizes that he may need time to become familiar with the adults, children, and activities in the class. She knows that this is Billy's first experience away from his parents. However, she is becoming concerned that his difficulties may be signs of special needs that require early intervention services. She decides to discuss her concerns with her program administrator, Mr. Clark, and to figure out how to discuss these observations with Billy's parents. Later that week, Evelyn and Mr. Clark meet with Mr. and Mrs. Patel to discuss Evelyn's observations. The Patels say that they have wondered about Billy's tendency to roam around and his lack of interest in other children at family gatherings. This is why they thought an early care setting would be good for him. They had hoped that Billy would become accustomed to Evelyn's class routine and become interested in other children. Mr. Clark explains the referral process for developmental screening and also describes early intervention services. The Patels say that no one else has ever mentioned these things to them. They express great relief to hear that Billy will receive the extra support he needs, and they thank Evelyn and Mr. Clark for their help.

As an experienced early childhood teacher, Evelyn was familiar with how much time most toddlers usually needed to become familiar with the class routine

and ways to help them feel comfortable, secure, and engaged in a new setting. She relies on her knowledge of child development to determine behaviors that seemed unusual and brings these concerns to the program administrator. Together they discuss their observations with Billy's parents and find out that his parents have also noticed these difficulties. Evelyn's experience demonstrates the important role that early childhood teachers play in identifying children who may need to be screened for developmental delays and for sharing information with families.

If the child is found to be eligible for early intervention services, other service providers may become involved with the child and family and may provide services in the early childhood setting. An individualized family service plan (IFSP) will be developed to address the child's special needs and the family's priorities and concerns. The following services may be provided:

- Family training, counseling, and home visits

- Special instruction

- Speech-language pathology services (sometimes referred to as speech therapy)

- Audiology services (hearing tests and hearing aids for children with hearing loss)

- Occupational therapy

- Physical therapy

- Psychological services

- Medical services (only for diagnostic or evaluation purposes)

- Health services needed to enable the child to benefit from the other services

- Social-work services

- Assistive technology devices (such as a communication device) and services

- Transportation

- Nutrition services

- Service coordination

Individualized Family Service Plan

When an infant is found to be eligible for early intervention services, an individualized family service plan (IFSP) must be developed. According to the Individuals with Disabilities Education Act (IDEA), the IFSP document should include the following elements:

1. The infant's current level of physical (fine and gross motor, vision, and hearing, and health), cognitive, communication, social or emotional, and adaptive (self-help) development

2. If the family agrees, information on the family's concerns, priorities, and resources related to the infant's development.

3. Main outcomes expected for the child, the criteria for accomplishment, timelines, and procedures for measuring progress

4. Specific early intervention services that will be provided and the frequency, intensity, and methods for delivering them

5. Natural environments in which early intervention services will be provided and, if applicable, justification for services that will not be provided in the natural environment

6. Initiation dates and duration of services

7. Name of the service coordinator who is qualified to implement and coordinate the IFSP with agencies and service providers

8. Steps to be taken to support the child's and family's transition from Part C services and to preschool or other services.

The IFSP is both a document and a process for providing appropriate and coordinated services to the child and family. The IFSP should be reviewed at least once every six months, and needed changes should be made. As a process, the IFSP facilitates collaboration with the family and service providers from various disciplines, outcomes that are valued by the family, and coordination of services from different agencies and service providers.

Teaming with Interpreters

When teachers and family members do not share a common language, teachers should collaborate with qualified interpreters so that the true meaning of eligibility categories and other early intervention terminology can be translated and explained to the family. Because early intervention terms are based on special education policy in the United States, they may not be easily translated from English to another language. There may not be a word-for-word translation, so the interpreter has to convey the accurate meaning of these terms. For example, words such as "developmentally appropriate practice," "early intervention," "inclusion," and "individualized family service plan" may require an explanation of their meaning when translated into another language. Moreover, if interpreters are not familiar with the beliefs and values on which early intervention services are based, they may provide inaccurate translations of relevant terminology. For instance, when asked how he translated the term "developmental delay, a Hmong interpreter said, "the child . . . cannot play with friends . . . cannot do anything" (Chen, Chan, and Brekken 1998).

This type of translation error can be avoided if teachers and early intervention service providers clarify terms with the interpreter in advance of the meeting. This example highlights the need for teachers and early intervention service providers to identify terms and concepts that need translation into the family's home language. Together with an interpreter, teachers and early intervention service providers may discuss the meaning of the terms and how best to communicate these concepts to families.

Gathering Information from Families

Begin by identifying information that is needed to help the child become comfortable in the early childhood setting. Figure out the best way to gather this information through conversations with the family. Develop a short list of questions to guide conversations. A sample format is provided.

Information About a New Child

Child's name _____ Date _____

Parent(s) _____

Teacher _____

Questions	Family Responses
1. What are your child's favorite times of day, activities, foods, things, and people?	
2. What activities, foods, and things does your child dislike?	
3. How does your child communicate?	
4. What seems to motivate his or her interactions with familiar people?	
5. What words does your child understand?	
6. What words does your child speak?	
7. Do you have any concerns about your child?	
8. Is there anything we should know that will help us in caring for him or her?	

Sharing Information with Families

Families of children with special needs may have concerns related to the extra time, attention, or particular supports that a child requires in an early childhood setting. Remember first that it is important to balance attentive listening with sharing information with the family. Initial visits to the program are valuable for introducing the child and family to the routines, activities, children, and adults in the early childhood setting. Use these opportunities to find out about the family's concerns and hopes for the child's participation in the group. Some families may be direct in their communication style and open about expressing concerns. Others may be more reserved and hesitate to ask questions.

Let the families know about the teacher–child ratio, who is likely to be their child's primary teacher, and address any concerns they may express. Ask about the family's preferred ways to keep in contact: by notes, e-mail, texting, phone calls, or brief discussions at drop-off and pickup times. Once the child attends the program, consider video recording the child's participation in daily activities. In this way the family can see how the child is doing in the group care setting.

Supporting Participation and a Sense of Belonging in the Early Care Setting

Once a child's special need has been identified and the appropriate services have been sought out within the early care setting, responsive teacher interactions are the essential foundation for supporting a child's participation and sense of belonging. Recommended practices in the Program for Infant/Toddler Care include individualization, adaptation, and being responsive to children and families. These practices are particularly significant when the child has a special need. For example, some infants and toddlers with special needs may benefit from encouragement to move their bodies and interact with toys and other children. A few easy-to-grasp, colorful objects can

Concerns of New Families Who Entrust Their Child to an Early Care Setting
New families often have many questions about an early care setting:

- How will my child behave in an unfamiliar place?
- Will my child be safe and happy?
- Will my child get the attention that he or she needs?
- Will my child get along with the other children?
- Will people like my child?

be displayed on low shelves of a neutral color so that the toys are easy for the children to see and reach. Infants who are not ambulatory may be placed on a mat with toys that are easy for them to grasp and tug. A child with a motor difficulty may be positioned with support (based on the physical therapist's recommendations) to facilitate rolling or reaching for toys. Some infants with developmental delays may appear passive and require more physical stimulation to maintain an alert state. Others may be become overly aroused or agitated by typical handling during caregiving activities (e.g., being held, fed, or diapered). A responsive teacher recognizes and responds to each child's particular signals. Discussing observations with the child's family and consulting relevant service providers (e.g., occupational therapist or physical therapist) may help teachers obtain suggestions necessary for engaging in sensitive ways with each child in their care.

Person-First Language

Another important way for child care program staff to be responsive to a child with special needs is to value the "child" as a child first and to avoid labeling the child as an eligibility category. For example, the phrase "a child with a developmental delay" should be used when referring to the child rather than "the developmentally delayed child." The terms (e.g., *developmental delay* or the name of a specific disability) are merely ones used to meet eligibility requirements for early intervention services and should not be used to stigmatize a child. Consider how the use of positive person-first language will promote a child's sense of identity, affect the family's feelings, and influence the expectations of children and adults who interact with the child and family.

Universal Design for Learning

Programs can be responsive to children with special needs by being sensitive to the principles of universal design for learning (UDL) that promote access to learning environments for children with a range of abilities through a variety of strategies that accommodate individual, cultural, and linguistic needs. The three principles of UDL involve multiple means of representation, expression, and engagement (CAST 2012).

Multiple means of representation refers to using a variety of formats that will enable children to acquire information. The range of formats may include English, home languages, manual signs, pictures, and objects. For example, to facilitate understanding, teachers may alert very young children about the next routine activity by using multiple means such as spoken words (in English and home languages), manual signs, pictures, or an object that represents the activity. A picture or object activity schedule may help toddlers anticipate familiar daily activities.

Multiple means of expression involves a range of ways for children to respond and to express preferences, feelings, and ideas. For example, children may indicate their preference for an activity by moving or pointing to the area, saying or signing a word, selecting a picture or object that represents the activity, or by pressing a voice output device or alternative and augmentative communication device (AAC).

During snack time, toddlers sit around a small table for a snack of crackers, cut-up fruit, and water. After the first serving, the care teacher waits for each child to communicate. Some children say "more," others "más," and one or two children make the sign for MORE or ALL DONE. The care teacher responds to each child's

communication in efforts to support each child's sense of identity and language development.

Multiple means of engagement captures children's attention by addressing their learning styles and interests and using scaffolds to support their participation. These scaffolds include identifying the characteristics of the objects and activities that the child prefers. For example, a toddler dislikes washing her hands but enjoys music time. The care teacher might encourage the child's participation by singing "This is the way we wash our hands . . . ."

Teaming with Early Intervention Service Providers

In an early care setting, a child with special needs may receive services from one or more early intervention service providers, such as a physical or occupational therapist, an early childhood special educator, and/or a speech and language pathologist. These early intervention service providers are likely to provide a consultation-based service delivery model. In this intervention model, service providers develop a partnership with the child's family and teachers to find out about the child's typical day, regular learning opportunities in the care setting, the child's preferred activities, and any challenges that tend to come up. It is essential for the child's early intervention team members (including teachers) and family members to discuss how to address the family's priorities and child's IFSP outcomes within the daily routine.

Embedding Specific Learning Opportunities in Daily Routines

Typical daily activities, such as playing with toys, eating a snack, or going for a

walk, are meaningful and natural opportunities for young children to develop and practice skills as they communicate and interact. These activities may be planned or may occur spontaneously. In collaboration with early intervention service providers, teachers should identify opportunities within the daily routines for targeting the child's learning need. For example, care teachers may target specific child behaviors such as pointing to objects or pictures or making a manual sign to indicate a choice during snack time.

Questions to Guide Practice

If a child receives early intervention services, teachers might ask the following questions:

1. What early intervention services will the child receive in the early care setting?

2. How are these services understood within the family's cultural perspective and linguistic background?

3. Who provides these services, what is involved, when will services be provided, and how will the child's early intervention services affect the typical day for the other children?

4. What information does the family, the teachers, and the service providers need to share to support this child's learning needs? How do they share that information?

5. Who will make the necessary modifications and supports for this child's participation?

6. What is expected of teachers beyond their usual roles and responsibilities?

7. How will early intervention service providers and teachers work together and collaborate with the family?

If the child's development or behavior causes concerns, determine:

1. What is the program procedure for discussing concerns with families?

2. What is the referral process for developmental screening?

Conclusion

Including young children with special needs in early care settings requires collaboration among families, teachers, and early intervention service providers. Adopting an open attitude of inquiry will enable teachers to develop a shared understanding of the child with the family. Teaming with early intervention service providers will promote the teachers' use of specific strategies to support children's participation in everyday learning opportunities. Early childhood teachers have a vital role in identifying infants and toddlers who may require developmental screenings and early intervention services. Teachers may also assist families in negotiating the unfamiliar and somewhat daunting system of early intervention. In this way, teachers may facilitate the positive developmental outcomes of young children with special needs as well as enhance their own partnerships with families of diverse cultural and linguistic backgrounds.

References

Center for Applied Special Technology (CAST). 2012. "Universal Design for Learning." http://www.cast.org/udl/index.html (accessed November 19, 2012).

Chen, D., S. Chan, and L. Brekken. 1998. *Conversations for Three: Communicating through Interpreters.* DVD. Van Nuys, CA: Child Development Media.

Cook, R. E., M. D. Klein, and D. Chen. 2012. *Adapting Early Childhood Curricula for Children with Special Needs.* 8th ed. Upper Saddle River, NJ: Pearson.

Lynch, E. W., and M. J. Hanson, eds. 2011. *Developing Cross-Cultural Competence: A Guide for Working with Children and Families.* 4th ed. Baltimore, MD: Paul H. Brookes.

U.S. Department of Education. 2011. *IDEA 2004: Building the Legacy. Part C (birth–2 years old).* http://www.idea.ed.gov/part-c/statutes (accessed November 19, 2012).

Section Two
Becoming Informed About
Cultural Practices and
Cultural Communities

A Cultural Communities and Cultural Practices Approach to Understanding Infant and Toddler Care

Alison Wishard Guerra and Sarah Garrity

A universal task in every society is to prepare children to engage in the community and contribute meaningfully to the family, community, and economy. How communities go about this, however, may be quite different. Often these differences are attributed to "cultural diversity," but what exactly defines one's culture? How can culture be seen? What sense can be made of culture? Culture is something in which everyone participates and can be seen as an ever-changing set of goals and activities that guide people's behavior and help to explain it. This chapter introduces culture as made up of "cultural communities" where people engage in shared "cultural practices" that represent the adaptive strategies developed by families for social and economic well-being (Rogoff 2003). The cultural communities and practices framework can serve as a way of thinking for providing culturally sensitive care to young children, especially in infant and toddler early care settings.

The cultural nature of development may be understood by thinking carefully about care practices and the functions and goals they serve. Those practices include both what people do as well as how they do them. For example, cultural practices include seemingly mundane routines such as eating and sleeping and the physical and cultural tools used in the routines (e.g., eating utensils, literacy or mathematics materials). An understanding of cultural practices needs to extend to the reasons and the goals for those routines.

Use of a cultural communities and practices framework to understand culture and development can help the early education and care field to move beyond two common assumptions that often cloud these discussions. The first assumption is that there is one set of "best practices" and one set of universal developmental goals for all children and families. By avoiding this static view and looking instead at culture as a fluid set of practices organized to accomplish specific goals, one sees that each cultural community may have a unique set of "best practices" and socialization and developmental goals for its children. All of these practices and goals are situated within the broader community context that includes political, social, and economic history.

The second assumption is that culture is equivalent to one's ethnic or linguistic background. Looking at culture as a set of practices rather than as a person's background provides a more powerful way to understand variations within ethnic and linguistic groups than simply comparing attributes across groups. As teachers, early care providers, and researchers often note, it is typical for more differences than similarities to appear among children from the same ethnic or linguistic backgrounds. Families from similar ethnic or linguistic backgrounds do not necessarily have the same routines, goals, or practices. Routines, goals, and practices are developed in the context of a family's history, including cultural and linguistic heritage, but they are usually more strongly associated with the immediate and recent social, political, and economic goals of the community.

The cultural practices, or routine ways of doing things, define the cultural context in which humans develop. Using this approach, practitioners and researchers can explore how culturally based practices with children drive developmental outcomes rather than focus exclusively on how developmental outcomes differ across ethnic and linguistic groups. The following vignette illustrates this concept.

Josue is a 17-month-old child whose family lives in an apartment in a large city located close to the Mexican border. His family has recently moved to the United States and has been living with his aunt and her four children. Josue has been attending a local infant/toddler program for almost two months. His teachers report that naptime is particularly difficult for Josue. Although obviously very tired, Josue struggles to transition to his cot and often lies on the floor and cries, which disturbs the other children and often wakes them. Josue's primary care teacher has tried carrying Josue to his cot and giving him a book or favorite toy to help him calm down; however, Josue rolls off the cot and onto the floor and continues to cry. When Josue finally does fall asleep, it is usually time for the children to get up and have a snack.

The lead teacher, Carla, decides to bring up this issue to her supervisor during her next reflective supervision meeting. When asked to describe how Josue's behavior during naptime makes her feel, Carla shares that she feels sad for Josue because he is so obviously distressed and that she wishes she could do something to help him. She also feels that since Josue has been in the program for almost two months, he should be able to make the transition to naptime more easily. When asked how Josue's behavior makes her feel in her role as lead teacher, Carla shares that she feels ineffective as a teacher and worries about the effect that Josue's behavior has on the other children. She also worries about how she and her assistant will get their lunch breaks since all children need to be asleep in order for one of them to leave the classroom. Carla's supervisor suggests that she do a home visit to get to know the family better and learn more about the family's caregiving routines.

During the home visit, Carla learns that Josue has slept with his mother since birth and that in Josue's country of origin, children typically sleep with a parent until another sibling is born, at which time they generally move to an older sibling's bed. When discussing this with her supervisor, Carla comes to understand that co-sleeping reflects a goal of Josue's cultural community, which is to foster interdependence.

As this vignette illustrates, the interdependence valued in Josue's home is dramatically different from the emphasis on self-reliance and autonomy found in his early care program. Researchers have reported that environments where sleep patterns are different from those of the home setting can lead to uncertainty for children (Provence, Naylor, and Patterson 1977) and that sleep patterns are often among the final practices to change when a family moves to a new country (Farooqui, Perry, and Beevers 1991). Josue experiences very different practices in the early care program, which are based on the goal of independence, from those he experiences at home. By making a home visit to learn more about family practices, Carla has taken an important first step toward understanding Josue's behavior and creating a sensitive and responsive classroom. In chapter 5, Janet Gonzalez-Mena further discusses efforts that teachers can make to understand the ways in which families engage in routine caregiving practices and to better serve the infants and toddlers in their care.

Participation in Cultural Practices at Home and in the Early Care Setting

The primary context for participation in cultural practices is typically the home, through social interactions and relationships with primary caregivers and other members of the community. However, most families participate in multiple cultural communities as they engage in neighborhood activities, spiritual activities, and with people of similar ethnic or linguistic backgrounds. For young infants and toddlers in early care settings, their cultural communities include, at a minimum, both the home and the child care context. An understanding of how culture informs interactions with children must

focus on the types of activities and the goals behind these activities in each of the child's cultural communities, primarily those of the home and the early care context.

Figure 4.1 provides a visual framework of how a family may participate in multiple cultural communities, each with a unique set of cultural practices designed to achieve the goals and values of the specific community. The family is depicted in the center, participating in each of four cultural communities that overlap to varying degrees. Other participants in each of these cultural communities may also participate in various cultural communities, creating both similarities and differences in practices, beliefs, and values.

Figure 4.1

Example of a Family Participating in Multiple Cultural Communities

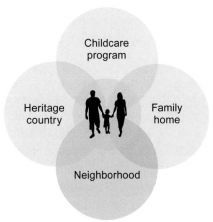

To summarize, this framework illustrates the cultural nature of development, both broadly conceived and specifically related to the context of infant/toddler learning environments. This framework will be used to define cultural communities and practices, discuss why they are relevant, and suggest how to think about

them. This approach will be applied to understand the family organization and highlight how variations in cultural practices in the family structure can have profound effects on children's development and their expectations for how the world works. This conceptual framework will be applied to the infant/toddler learning environment and to the infant/toddler care teacher's interactions with children and families. The discussion will illuminate how the infant/toddler learning environment can be seen as its own cultural community with unique cultural practices, specific to the historical and current needs, values, and goals of the community.

Understanding Cultural Communities

Within the cultural community perspective, *culture* refers to participation in cultural processes that unite groups of people into communities. In this sense, a cultural community is a group of people who share a set of core practices aimed at accomplishing certain things together, with attention to the way they coordinate their activities and relate to each other (Rogoff 2003). Rogoff defines *communities* as "groups of people who have some common and continuing organization, values, understanding, history, and practices" (2003, 80).

Members of cultural communities often share a common racial, ethnic, national, geographic, linguistic, or historical identity, but the defining feature of all cultural communities is evolving, shared *practices.* Moreover, individuals typically participate in multiple cultural communities, sharing beliefs and practices maintained in different communities that reflect the multifaceted nature of their own history, values, and goals for their family. Consider, for example, two families connected to a military-connected community whose children are enrolled in the same program. While they may share many common experiences and beliefs based their on participation in this community, participation in their racial, ethnic, geographic, or linguistic communities will also shape their goals for their children.

Cultural communities are neither fixed in time nor a geographic place; instead, they reflect the changing demographics of the community and needs of the participants. Although cultural communities adapt their practices to the changing times, they also include practices from previous generations that may or may not continue to be relevant. Routine caregiving practices often continue even after social and economic circumstances have changed. For example, across many different ethnic and linguistic groups, adults maintain the practice of spoon-feeding their children despite the children's physical ability to use utensils and the presence of an adequate food supply. This practice, which ensures that food is not wasted, may have been carried over from a time when there was a limited food supply.

Likewise, the cultural concept of community is not limited to people in a specific geographic area with regular face-to-face contact. Rather, a cultural community spanning geographic regions can activate networks of family and community members, coordinating social and economic resources to accomplish a shared set of goals. In terms of early care, a relevant example of a cultural community that spans geographic regions is that of a family who recently immigrated from another country, where they continue to share social and economic resources with community members in their home country. The goals and practices of the cultural community in the home country continue to guide the daily practices of the members living in the new country in similar and new and unique ways (Howes, Wishard Guerra, and Zucker 2007). Such cultural communities that span geographic areas, as well as the individuals participating in those communities, are not static and continue to change in response to changing circumstances, values, and goals.

Use of a cultural communities approach to understand the infant/toddler care context may facilitate humanistic connections across ethnic and linguistic groups by emphasizing the role of shared goals and practices that define different cultural communities. In this approach, an infant/toddler care program provides a context in which parents, families, and early care providers from different ethnic heritage backgrounds may band together in sharing similar goals for the children and the community and in determining a unique set of practices to accomplish those goals. By relating to culture as a set of practices, infant/toddler programs can validate that humans are not bound to the culture they were born into, but rather actively participate in and develop their cultural community.

Understanding Cultural Practices

The common ways of doing things that describe and distinguish individual cultural communities are cultural practices. Cultural practices are routine activities that have a shared meaning among a group of individuals (Howes, Wishard Guerra, and Zucker 2007; Miller and Goodnow 1995; Rogoff 2003). Cultural practices include ways of ensuring economic sustainability, family structures, and social networks. Specifically relevant to the infant/toddler care setting are everyday child-rearing practices, such as the way a mother responds to her child's distress and the choice to use relative or nonrelative child care when the mother or father is not available to care for the child. As a result of shared practices, participants in cultural communities, especially those based in shared ethnic, racial, and language identities, often have common social interaction styles and parenting practices (Garcia Coll et al. 1996; Howes, Wishard Guerra, and Zucker 2007).

Using a culture and communities and practices framework can help early care providers understand culture as dynamic and avoid stereotypes in which all people in a group are assumed to live the same lifestyle and have the same goals for their children. Likewise, it can be seen that the child care setting may become its own cultural community, with a set of shared practices and ways of doing things, and that this cultural community has a profound impact on the participating children and adults.

Families and Communities

The way families organize everyday caregiving routines is driven both by the availability of caregivers within families, the organization of families' dwellings, and the socialization goals and values that families have for the children. From a cultural community practices perspective, these factors contribute to essential cultural practices, including caregiving routines. Caregiving practices and family organization may look dramatically different in different cultural communities across the world. Many of these differences are related to the varying rates of infant mortality, economic constraints, the availability of siblings and other family members to provide care, and cultural practices relating to engaging in groups or dyads (Rogoff 2003).

Variations in Caregiving Arrangements

The nature of a child's relationship with primary caregivers guides the way children develop relationships with others and influences how children learn. For many years, doctors and developmental scientists believed that children's primary attachment relationships were only with their primary caregiver, most often the mother, and that it was this one relationship that organized the way a child interacted with other adults and children. More recently, researchers of attachment and culture have suggested that the ways children form attachment relationships, as well as the people they form attachment relationships with, can be understood only within the context of the cultural community (Howes and Wishard Guerra 2009; Rothbaum et al. 2000).

Although the primary caregiving relationship in many homes is between the mother and child, this structure is not the norm for many families across the world. For many families, there is a network of primary caregivers who provide care to the child either in a one-on-one setting or with multiple caregivers and often multiple children present. There may be a wide variety of caregivers in a wide variety of settings and social groups: from relatives to child care providers, and from dyadic caregiving interactions to larger-group caregiving interactions. The presence of multiple caregivers does not interfere with a child's ability to form a trusting relationship with his or her mother or parent; in fact, the presence of multiple secure and trusting attachment relationships can help protect young children from the stresses of daily life related to family poverty, emotional trauma, or parental stress among others (Spieker et al. 2003). Each caregiver who provides physical and emotional care, continuity, or consistency in the child's life and has an emotional investment in the child is thought to be identified as an attachment figure for an infant or young child (Howes 1999; Howes and Smith 1995). Secure relationships with additional attachment figures, including teachers and child caregivers, can at least partially compensate for insecure parent–child relationships (Howes et al. 1988; Mitchell-Copeland, Denham, and DeMulder 1997;

Spieker et al. 2003; Wishard et al. 2003). Each attachment figure provides the child with an opportunity to develop a close, positive relationship that can serve as a secure base for exploring the world.

Siblings as caregivers. In many communities, infant and toddler care is primarily provided by five- to 10-year-old siblings or community children (Edwards and Whiting 1993; Harkness and Super 1992, LeVine et al. 1994; Rogoff 2003). In those communities, caregiving practices may be split into those pertaining to playing with and entertaining children, and those pertaining to teaching basic skills and feeding, changing, and bathing. Often the infants and toddlers are brought to the adults only when they need feeding, changing, or bathing and left to the siblings and older children for play, entertainment, and teaching of basic skills. For example, in Mexican working-class families, children are rarely seen playing with their mothers; instead, they play primarily with older children in a mixed-age context. In these types of arrangements, the quality and complexity of the peer play often resembles the nature of play observed in U.S. mother–child play (Farver 1992; 1993). Similarly, one study found that children in a working-class African American community in the Carolinas tended to watch and listen to adults and played and talked to other children. Older children often engaged in song, language play, counting, naming of items, and other activities with babies—activities typically engaged in by *adults* in middle-class European American communities (Heath 1993; Rogoff 2003).

Same-age peers versus mixed-age peers. When infants and toddlers have access to larger groups of children, whether siblings, other relatives, or other children in the community, they typically play in mixed-age groups. In fact, grouping children according to age is relatively unusual around the world, where sibling relationships are prioritized over peer relationships. In many North American families, however, peer relationships are prioritized over sibling relationships, and children are separated from siblings in same-age classroom settings.

In North American families with few siblings or other children available, young children are often separated in same-age groups of infants and toddlers, preschoolers, and school-age children. Certainly this is also the pattern in most child care centers where classrooms and programs are designed to meet the needs of a narrow age range of children. When infants and toddlers first arrive at a child care program, the child may feel more comfortable in a mixed-age setting and seek playtime and affection from older siblings or older children at the center rather than

from unfamiliar adult teachers. As care teachers seek to provide culturally sensitive care, it is important to ask the families about who participates in the everyday caregiving, including feeding, changing, bathing, and playing. For those children, providing them with time to play with older children may be an important factor in assisting in their social–emotional adjustment. Of course, when infants and toddlers are cared for in family child care homes, play with older children happens naturally throughout the day.

The community as caregiver. In many communities, the primary responsibility of child supervision may belong to the general cultural community rather than to the individual parents. In these settings, children may expect any number of adults to engage in daily care routines, and the children may move fluidly back and forth between nonrelative community caregivers and relative or parent caregivers.

In North America and many industrialized nations where one or more parents work outside the home, the early care setting has come to serve as a "community as caregiver" model, where children are brought to the community center to be cared for by a cultural community of "expert" caregivers, engaging in specific cultural practices with the goal of providing care and support to young children. It is useful to consider the early care setting from the cultural communities' perspective. This enables one to view the daily routines and practices as an organized system of practices geared toward achieving very specific goals. When these cultural practices and goals conflict with those of the attending children and families, the transition from home to center can be strained, potentially weakening the connection between the family and the child care providers. To

minimize potential conflict between the home and the center, care programs need to establish open communication and collaboration with families. Though family child care may be more consonant with families' cultural practices and goals, open communication and collaboration are just as important.

Children's involvement in mature activities. The degree to which children are either included in or separated from adult activities varies according to the nature of the caregiving routines. When children are raised in cultural communities where child-rearing is considered more of a communal event, children are often included in the mature activities of the community and given small but authentic tasks that contribute to the community. The practice of giving children "toys" and filling their day with child-oriented activities may be common only in industrialized nations, where children are often segregated from mature adult activities and grouped into same-age peer groups for care. However, some approaches to early childhood education, such as those developed by Maria Montessori, argue that young children, especially infants and toddlers, are most

interested in engaging in the everyday activities they see the adults in their community participate in. According to such approaches, activities related to "practical life" are seen as especially suited to children's interests and developmental abilities. Allowing young children to participate in real tasks relating to the care of the environment, such as sweeping, dusting, watering plants, and food preparation can be a wonderful and meaningful way to include them in the everyday practices of the child care community. And when young children give care to babies, the babies experience firsthand how their older peers contribute to the community.

In sum, the caregiving practices within the family and community are deeply connected to the family structure, the social and economic structures and demands of the community, and the historical goals for young children's socialization. The early care program, particularly centers, may present a stark difference from the everyday caregiving routines a young infant or toddler is familiar with. Consequently, the program may potentially increase the stress associated with separa-

tion from the child's primary caregiver. A cultural communities and cultural practices framework provides a tangible way for caregivers to understand how culture shapes children's development and the goals of parents and families for their children. By tuning in to the cultural practices of families who attend the child care program, child care providers may be better able to create and sustain a cultural community within the program by including cultural practices that respect and support the practices that children and families may be familiar with.

Interactions with Children and Families and Becoming Informed About Cultural Practices and Cultural Communities

By inviting families to share their caregiving practices, early care providers can work with families to develop care routines that reflect the practices of the home cultural community and thereby decrease cultural conflict for children. To create such partnerships, however, teachers need to be flexible, because often the practices used by families may greatly differ from current practices in early care and education programs.

Program policies, such as attendance and continuity of care, illustrate how program goals and practices might conflict with parental goals and practices. During the summer months, enrollment and/or attendance may go down as older siblings who are home from school for the summer may care for infants and toddlers. Although this may disrupt the continuity of care and the developing relationship between the infant/toddler care teacher and other children, the practice of older siblings caring for younger ones may be an important caregiving practice passed

on from previous generations. When school is out for the summer and older siblings are available, families may prefer to adhere to their value that the youngest members (infants and toddlers) be cared for within the cultural community rather than by outside experts. As this example of attendance during the summer months suggests, keeping children home may reflect the community goals related to the interdependence of family members and a history of children being cared for by older members of the community in mixed age groups.

Infant/toddler care teachers must use their understanding of cultural practices and cultural communities to inform their interactions with children and families. To do this requires ongoing critical thinking, reflection, and the ability to take the perspective of others with differing orientations. Sensoy and DiAngelo (2012) call attention to the need to distinguish opinions, which are a product of collective socialization and do not require critical thinking, from uninformed knowledge, which is the result of ongoing experience and study. In contrast to opinions, uninformed knowledge requires individuals to expand, question, and go beneath the surface of initial ideas to truly learn about the goals, ideologies, and practices enacted by various cultural communities and how they relate to caregiving practices. Such an approach leads to exploration of many questions; for instance, how might a history of food shortage (or the opposite experience of having food in abundance) affect the practices associated with feeding? (See chapter 5 to further explore routine caregiving practices associated with feeding.) Or how might various cultural communities view the teaching and learning process? Without critical thinking and reflection, conflicts between programs and communities may emerge that understanding and open communication of goals and practices could have minimized or prevented. Consideration of what will influence teacher practice requires asking the following questions:

1. How does the family balance the goals of independence and interdependence for children?

2. Is it the goal of the caregiver to prepare the environment or to have children to participate in the preparing the environment or both?

3. Is it the goal of the program for the children to participate in the mature activities of the community or to play, or to do some of both?

By learning from the families their caregiving goals, one can focus on under-

standing them. Exploring the reasons why certain goals are preferred reveals the history and assumptions behind typical care routines enacted by both the cultural communities served and the early care and education program.

Understanding the Classroom or Program as Its Own Cultural Community

Just as teachers need to respond sensitively to the various temperaments, languages, and dispositions of children in their care, so they must also respond thoughtfully to the various caregiving practices used by members of different cultural communities. Participation in cultural communities is fluid, and individuals and families often participate in several cultural communities at the same time. As families participate in multiple sets of cultural practices, they are often able to better understand the goals and values maintained within each community. Through open communication and collaboration with families, teachers and program directors can build their understanding of multiple sets of caregiving practices to create a cultural community reflective and supportive of the various sets of cultural practices that the children are familiar with.

Children develop through guided participation in cultural practices and daily routines. By understanding the concept of multiple sets of cultural practices, teachers can, for example, find ways to both support continuity of primary caregivers to children and, at the same time, effectively provide culturally relevant and sensitive care. By considering the early care program as a cultural community with its own set of unique cultural practices, teachers can both

borrow practices from other cultural communities and build on cultural traditions of the families enrolled in the program as well as the people living in the geographic region. For example, programs serving children who are accustomed growing up in mixed-age groups and participating in the daily activities of adults may decide to adopt a schedule allowing the infants and toddlers to share some routines with older children, such as mealtime, play time, and participation in practical life activities such as caring for the environment. They may also gain ideas by visiting and observing nearby family child care programs.

A community practices framework is a pragmatic approach to culture to aid in understanding the specific aspects of family life that are relevant to the early care environment. This approach results in a culturally sensitive early care environment that both acknowledges the cultural communities of incoming families and develops new cultural practices.

In conclusion, there is great variation in the care of infants and toddlers. Sensitive and responsive teachers should seek information about community practices and integrate them into the cultural community of their program. Integration of cultural practices requires ongoing critical thinking, wondering, and reflection as teachers learn from families and the larger community about the goals and values held for children and the practices that reflect those goals. By doing so, meaningful and authentic collaboration between parents and teachers develops, which in turn builds an infant/toddler care community that supports the cultural goals and caregiving practices of families.

References

Edwards, C. P., and B. B. Whiting. 1993. "'Mother, Older Sibling and Me': The Overlapping Roles of Caregivers and Companions in the Social World of Two- to Three-Year-Olds in Ngeca, Kenya." In *Parent-Child Play: Descriptions and Implications*, edited by K. MacDonald, 305–28. Albany: State University of New York Press.

Farooqui, S. I., J. Perry, and D. G. Beevers. 1991. "Ethnic Differences in Sleeping Position and Risk of Cot Death." *The Lancet* 338:1445.

Farver, J. A. M. 1992. "An Analysis of Young American and Mexican Children's Play Dialogues." In *The Collaborative Construction of Pretend*, edited by C. Howes, 55–66. Albany: State University of New York Press.

——1993. "Cultural Differences in Scaffolding Pretend Play: A Comparison of American and Mexican Mother–Child and Sibling–Child Pairs." In *Parent-Child Play: Descriptions and Implications,* edited by K. MacDonald. Albany: State University of New York Press.

Garcia Coll, C., K. Crnic, G. Lamberty, B. Wasik, R. Jenkins, H. Garcia Vazquez, and H. Pipes McAdoo. 1996. "An Integrative Model for the Study of Developmental Competencies in Minority Children." *Child Development* 67 (5): 1891–1914.

Harkness, S., and C. M. Super. 1992. "The Developmental Niche: A Theoretical Framework for Analyzing the Household Production of Health." *Social Science and Medicine* 38 (2): 217–26.

Heath, S. B. 1993. *Identity and Inner-City Youth: Beyond Ethnicity and Gender.* New York: Teachers College Press.

Howes, C. 1999. "Attachment Relationships in the Context of Multiple Caregivers." In *Handbook of Attachment: Theory, Research, and Clinical Applications,* edited by J. Cassidy and P. R. Shaver, 671–87.

Howes, C., and A. Wishard Guerra. 2009. "Networks of Attachment Relationships in Low-Income Children of Mexican Heritage: Infancy through Preschool." *Social Development* 18 (4): 896–914.

Howes, C., A. Wishard Guerra, and E. Zucker. 2007. "Cultural Communities and Parenting in Mexican-Heritage Families." *Parenting: Science and Practice* 7 (3): 235–70.

Howes, C., C. Rodning, D. C. Galuzzo, and L. Myers. 1988. "Attachment and Child Care: Relationships with Mother and Caregiver." *Early Childhood Research Quarterly* 3:403–16.

Howes, C., and E. W. Smith. 1995. "Children and Their Child Care Caregivers: Profiles of Relationships. *Social Development* 4:44–61.

LeVine, R. A., S. Dixon, S. LeVine, A. Richman, , P. H. Leiderman, C. H. Keefer, and T. B. Brazelton. 1994. *Child Care and Culture: Lessons from Africa.* New York: Cambridge University Press.

Miller, P. J., and J. J. Goodnow. 1995. "Cultural Practices: Toward an Integration of Culture and Development." *New Directions for Child Development* 67:5–16.

Mitchell-Copeland, J., S. A. Denham, and E. K. DeMulder 1997. "Q-Sort Assessment of Child–Teacher Attachment Relationships and Social Competence in the Preschool." *Early Education & Development* 8 (1): 27–39.

Parlakian, R. 2001. *Look, Listen, and Learn: Reflective Supervision and Relationship-Based Work.* Washington, DC: Zero to Three.

Provence, S., A. Naylor, and J. Patterson. 1977. *The Challenge of Day Care.* New Haven, CT: Yale University Press.

Rogoff, B. 2003. *The Cultural Nature of Human Development.* New York: Oxford University Press.

Rothbaum, F., M. Pott, H. Azuma, K. Miyake, and J. Weisz. 2000. "The Development of Close Relationships in Japan and the United States: Paths of Symbiotic Harmony and Generative Tension." *Child Development* 71:1121–42.

Sensoy, O., and R. DiAngelo. 2012. *Is Everyone Really Equal? An Introduction to Key Concepts in Social Justice Education.* New York: Teachers College Press.

Spieker, S. J., D. C. Nelson, A. Petras, S. N. Jolley, and K. E. Barnard. 2003. "Joint Influence of Child care and Infant Attachment Security for Cognitive and Language Outcomes of Low-Income Toddlers." *Infant Behavior & Development* 26 (3): 326–44.

Wishard, A., E. M. Shivers, C. Howes, and S. Ritchie. 2003. "Child Care Programs and Teacher Practices: Associations with Quality and Children's Experiences." *Early Childhood Research Quarterly* 18:65–103.

Cultural Sensitivity in Caregiving Routines: The Essential Activities of Daily Living

Janet Gonzalez-Mena

Every day you bring your personal values and beliefs to your work with children and families, and it is likely that the way you were raised shaped those beliefs and values. Therefore, it is essential to understand just how cultural upbringing influences child care practice. Interactions you engaged in, even during your own infancy, around such basic activities as feeding, toileting, and napping had an effect on what you may think is the right way to care for children and will even influence the specific caregiving

techniques you use. Additionally, your practice is influenced by the way you were trained as an infant/toddler care teacher. Therefore, it is important to understand that you come to child care with both a conscious and not-so-conscious set of beliefs, values, and rules for behavior that come from your history and training. When you work with families that were raised in ways different from you and hold different beliefs and values about child-rearing, it is crucial to be aware that both sets of beliefs may be valid.

When caring for infants and toddlers, remember that you are participating in a subtle, but powerful form of teaching. The way care—the everyday caregiving activities you engage in over and over again—is provided has a profound effect on early development. While engaging in routine tasks, teachers pass on important messages about how life should be lived. Personal and cultural values are reflected in the way you provide care. If the child-rearing practices of the parents of the infants and toddlers in your care are not in agreement with yours, you may wind up socializing a child in a manner contrary to what a parent wants. This chapter is written to lessen that possibility.

Differing Beliefs and Values

Many times, infant/toddler care teachers are unaware of what parents are trying to accomplish—the values behind a request—when the parents ask for a routine to be done in a particular way. For example, parents who endorse caregiving practices that stress self-help skills and competence building in infants, such as feeding oneself and putting oneself to sleep alone in a crib, usually want their children to grow up to be self-sufficient, and they tend to think the time to start is in infancy. The goal behind those practices often is to produce an independent, unique individual. In contrast to that goal, some parents feel a child's sense of belonging to a group may be more important than independence. These parents see optimum functioning in the group or family system as a greater priority than independence; therefore, their child-rearing practices emphasize group experience. These parents may expect adults and older children to help a child with eating throughout early childhood and consider falling asleep to be something the child always does in the presence of others. Parents who endorse those practices tend to value the goal of interdependence more than that of independence. Although it may seem like families face an "either/or" situation, in reality some families fall somewhere in between the goals of independence and interdependence.

Both goals are valid. Yet the difference between them is fundamental. If a teacher can conduct a routine in a way that allows both goals to be met, it is the optimal outcome for all. Routine caregiving practices carried out with attention to parents' preferences will allow teachers to acknowledge, work with, and resolve potential conflicts or "cultural bumps" as Isaura Barrera calls them. They invariably arise when people hold different viewpoints. Only with this flexibility can one truly provide infants and toddlers with the sensitive care that supports their

development within their family and cultural context. This approach is consistent with Alison Wishard Guerra and Sarah Garrity's guidance in chapter 4, which recommends the use of a cultural communities framework to help teachers understand parents' goals for their children.

What Is a Routine?

There are several different uses of the word *routine.* Although most people do not admit that routines are repetitive and boring, they often perceive them as such. Furthermore, people often have different ideas about what the word actually means. Once I overheard a participant leaving my workshop complain to someone that the workshop was over, and she was leaving without having gotten a routine to take away with her. I was curious about what she had expected from the workshop until I found out that she had expected to leave with a schedule in hand that specified what routine to do and when.

At another time a woman attending my workshop, who was native to the North American continent and called herself an Indian, talked to me at length about the preschool her child attended. She complained about how the teachers always looked at their watches and then at the schedule on the wall. That practice upset her because it was unlike her child's experience at home. Furthermore, the message she received from the preschool was that she was supposed to have a schedule at home for her children to replace the daily free-flow that felt right and natural to her. She went on to point out that the words for the schedule all had the word "time": as in "arrival time," "outdoor time," "snack time." Furthermore, time may be important in some cultures and not so in others; even the

concept of time may cause confusion and sometimes cause hard feelings or discomfort. That was the case when the mother thought she was supposed to use time segments to regulate her day at home instead of allowing a more free-flowing daily routine.

In her book *Respecting Babies,* Ruth Anne Hammond puts a "positive spin" on the word *routine* as it applies to the daily life of infants and toddlers:

> *Routine is a pathway . . . that provides a framework so that each day need not be a new invention, but is an opportunity to fine tune one's orientation to the world. It takes on the spirit of beloved ritual that nurtures relationships as much as bodies.* (Hammond 2009, 46)

Cultural Differences in Daily Routines: Toileting, Feeding, and Sleeping/Napping

You will probably be unfamiliar with some of the positions people hold about toileting, feeding, and sleeping/napping due to their cultural background. You may even be unaware of your own values connected with them until you find yourself in a conflict with a parent or a fellow infant/toddler care teacher about one of them.

Consider these three situations and think about your probable response:

1. *Toileting.* A new parent explains to you that her one-year-old child is toilet trained and insists that you leave off the diapers.

2. *Feeding.* The mother of a toddler is upset by the mess she sees when she discovers that you let him feed himself. She asks you to spoon-feed her child as she does at home, "so he eats more, doesn't get so messy, and less food is wasted."

3. *Napping.* Another parent explains that his baby is used to falling asleep in someone's arms, not by herself in a crib in a separate room. He asks that you hold the child until she goes to sleep each day.

Now reflect on your process. When you considered the three scenarios, was your natural inclination to think about such things as your program policies, philosophy, guidelines, developmental theory, research studies, or even licensing regulations? If so, you acted as most teachers would. Teachers often raise such issues in responding to a parent who asks for something to be done differently from the child care program's standard routine, especially when the request is for something that seems unreasonable and difficult to carry out.

Child care programs in family homes and centers are serving an increasingly diverse population. Parents may or may not have chosen your program because of its philosophy and caregiving practices.

It is vital to find out how the parents view their child's care and the practices related to it. Observe. Ask. Good communication with parents is the key to providing the best care for each infant or toddler. Communication is especially important in a culturally diverse program. This chapter examines three caregiving routines.

Toileting

Most experts (e.g., Sears, Brazelton, and the American Academy of Pediatrics) agree that to start toilet training much before two years of age is unwise. In their view, the child's readiness is the main factor in deciding when to start toilet training. This readiness involves the child's physical, intellectual, and emotional abilities to control, understand, and cooperate in the toilet-training or toilet-learning process. The goal of toileting, in the experts' approach, is to get children to handle their own toileting without adult help. For that reason, a child must be mature enough to walk, talk, handle clothing, and so forth. Toilet training, or toilet learning, is considered an important step in the child's growing independence.

As sensible as the experts' approach to toileting may appear, there are other points of view on the matter. For some parents, the goal of toileting is to create a partnership between parent and child; these parents may also want to eliminate the use of diapers as early as possible. Eventually, the self-help skills and independence in toileting will come, but that development is not seen as necessary or important to begin the toilet-training process.

Janice Hale, a professor at Wayne State University and author of many books about the African American child, talks about an approach to toilet training that is different from the experts' wait-until-two-years-of-age approach. Hale states that in some cultural communities, babies are held so much of the time that teachers can give "an immediate response to urination and bowel movements. Hence, from an early age, there is an association in the infant's mind between these functions and action from the mother. Consequently, when the mother seeks to toilet train the child, the child is accustomed to her direct involvement in this process" (Hale 1983, 70).

Hale pointed out that difference in toileting many years ago. Much more recently, Spock and Needlman (2011) introduced an idea they call "early toilet training," which can occur in the first year. What they explain as "early toilet training" relates in some ways to what some parents call "elimination communication." These parents are using the same idea that some African American families (and other families around the world) have been using for centuries. The Web site http://www.diaperfreebaby.com/ boldly declares that elimination communication is not potty training.

How is it different? The widely accepted process backed by experts that is called "potty training" or "toilet learning" comes after a long period, when babies' bodily functions of elimination typically occur when they are physically separate from the parent or caregiver(s). The parent or caregiver begins to become actively involved in the child's bowel and bladder activities after many months of giving them only cursory attention. A toilet-training or toilet-learning process based on readiness, beginning when the caregiver perceives that the child is ready for it, is very different from an ongoing process based on a partnership between a caregiver and child who maintain close physical contact with one another.

If a mother is sensitive to her one-year-old's signals and manages the child's toileting without diapers, it is quite reasonable for her to ask the child's teacher to do the same. Her expectations may be that the teacher will form the same kind of partnership that she and her infant have developed together. Therefore, when she talks about the child being toilet trained, she does not mean that the child will go to the bathroom and use the toilet independently. She means that the teacher will be able to read the child's signals and take the child to the toilet.

Teachers who have experience with children from a variety of backgrounds know that many young babies often do not have wet diapers. That observation supports the idea that an early adult–child partnership and early toileting are possible. Whether or not a particular toileting practice is advocated, it is necessary to know that variations in children's responses to toileting may reflect a cultural or family difference rather than a physical difference. The infant's capability for early toileting comes from continual physical contact with the caregiver and the caregiver's belief that dry diapers are possible, even for babies.

Communicating About Toileting

Understanding that a parent may have a different view of toileting because of cultural or individual beliefs and practices is crucial when communicating about different approaches. In the following scenario, notice the miscommunication that occurs:

The mother arrives to pick up her 12-month-old son and finds him playing on the floor, in a wet diaper, while the teacher is busy fixing the afternoon snack.

The mother frowns as she carries her son over to the diapering table and changes him. Her displeasure shows on her face throughout the process, but she does not say anything until she is on her way out the door. Then, as a parting remark, the mother says over her shoulder to the teacher, "I wish you'd be more alert and catch my son before he wets! At home he stays dry because he's toilet trained." "Sure he's trained!" the teacher says sarcastically under her breath, as though she does not believe it. Then she adds, loudly enough for the mother to hear, "He's not trained. You are!"

The parent and the teacher have a problem. Obviously, there has been no prior communication about the parent's expectations about toileting, dry diapers, and the like. The teacher has not talked with the parent about the child care program's expectations or what is reasonable for a parent to expect when his or her child is being cared for in a group setting. Another problem is the attitude of nonacceptance expressed by both the teacher and the parent toward each other's caregiving practices.

If you were in the teacher's shoes, you might have difficulty following that parent's practice, even if you wanted to. You might feel you could not possibly hold one baby all the time in order to learn the subtle body signals the baby sends just before he or she wets. How could you possibly take care of more than one infant and hold each one all the time? But if you understand the mother's experience, her point of view, and her definition of toilet training, your attitude toward her will be different from just thinking of her as lacking knowledge.

The parent, too, might have a more accepting attitude of you and your caregiving practices if you had arranged a conversation with her about the difference between caring for infants and toddlers in groups and caring for one baby alone at home. That conversation between the parent and teacher needs to begin *before* the child is in care, during a parent–teacher orientation. The discussion between parents and teachers is a two-way street. In addition to sharing information, the mother and teacher need to engage in some problem solving about consistency of care and shared expectations for the child's care.

You may be surprised, as I have been, that some teachers work with families who use an elimination communication

approach, and teachers say it can work—even in group care settings! I have not tried it myself, but I see the advantages of being so tuned in to a baby—so observant, so sensitive—that you get to know that baby very well. Imagine what it must feel like to be that baby.

Feeding Practices

Cultural differences often arise when breast-feeding is concerned. Programs serving families of infants and toddlers tend to support families in their choice to breast-feed or not (Liamputtong 2011). Programs may offer mothers a quiet, secluded place to breast-feed and a proper storage space for breast milk so it can be fed to their infants in bottles when the mother is not available. Cultural differences also arise in the timing of introducing solid foods and the expectations about how feeding is handled.

The focus of this section is feeding infants and toddlers solid food in child care programs. A major issue arises around the fact that self-feeding of very young children is a messy but an important step toward independence. According to the experts—Brazelton and Sparrow, for example—it is important to encourage babies to take part in the feeding process, even though a mess results. Some experts even suggest that babies be allowed to play with their food to get the full benefit of the sensory experience. Almost everyone who has been involved in infant/toddler child care has been confronted with a parent who is unhappy about a mess. Moreover, some teachers may be uncomfortable with messes as well.

There may be several reasons why some parents or some caregivers object to allowing babies to feed themselves, even when they are capable of doing so.

Some cultural practices forbid fingers from ever touching food. In some cultural communities, food is revered and is never considered a play thing at the table or as an activity, such as finger painting with pudding. Parents or caregivers who have experienced severe food shortages or who empathize with the circumstances of starvation may be horrified at the thought of playing with food.

When there is a core belief about the importance of cleanliness, experiences with the tactile properties of food and playing with food are discouraged. Parents who have little time to feed their babies or who clean them afterwards may find that spoon-feeding them until they can eat neatly and efficiently by themselves is more expedient, even though some children may reach that point as late as four years of age. Telling parents about the importance of taking time to feed their children is easy enough, but many will not hear the message because they have a different set of priorities and values. However, in the early care setting there is time for children to learn self-feeding skills and for adults to clean up the mess. Again, it is important to recognize that values and beliefs are what drive caregiv-

ing practices; feeding practices need to be discussed in the parent/caregiver orientation meeting and in conversations.

Marion Cowee, a preschool teacher–director in the San Francisco Bay Area, tells about her experience with a mother spoon-feeding her child beyond infancy. When a Chinese family enrolled, Marion was surprised to discover that the mother was still spoon-feeding her four-year-old daughter. In fact, she came at lunch time each day for that very purpose. When Marion asked her why she did it, the mother replied, "To make sure my daughter is getting enough to eat." Marion thought she was overprotective and gently tried to convince the mother that her child was old enough to feed herself. She also shared with the mother her worries about the child's lack of self-help skills in kindergarten, but the mother never quit coming at lunch time. In spite of their different views about the need for self-help skills, they developed a positive relationship. By the end of the school year, nothing had changed at lunch time. A year later, the mother and daughter came back to visit Marion at the preschool. After a warm, get-reacquainted conversation, Marion asked about how lunch time was at school. The mother proudly announced that she had gotten a job as a lunch-room supervisor, so she knew that her child got enough to eat. By then she had stopped spoon-feeding her.

Marion's comments about this story were as follows: "This experience taught me how powerful cultural practices are; it's not something that can be willed away by logic or guilt." She went on to say, "By a unilateral decree on my part, I could have forced an important part of a family's link to their cultural community to be absent in my program. By doing that, I might have destroyed the trust and

joy that that family experienced in our school" (Cowee 2012).

Sleeping/Napping Routines

As in feeding and toileting routines, different cultural and personal values support different practices related to sleeping and napping. But being open to cultural variation in sleeping practices has become highly sensitive since the back-to-sleep movement changed infant sleeping practices in many cultural communities. One outcome of the movement is the lowering of the risk factors of SIDS (sudden infant death syndrome) and that is a blessing. Yet the American Academy of Pediatrics recommendation against co-sleeping bumps up against the infant sleeping practices in many cultures. Taking a different perspective from that of the American Academy of Pediatrics, sleep scientist James McKenna (2000), and an anthropologist, Meredith Small (1998), as well as Sears and Sears (2001 and 2003), find some co-sleeping practices benefit babies and lower SIDS risk factors. Decisions should be made carefully here.

Sears and Sears (2001 and 2003) give recommendations for safe co-sleeping, which include putting the baby on his back and guarding against overheating. They list a number of "don'ts," which include drugs, alcohol, smoking, and soft surfaces (such as beanbag chairs and waterbeds) as well hair spray, deodorants, and perfumes. Obesity of the adults is another risk factor.

One thing is clear, however: the idea that babies should sleep in separate cribs in a quiet room away from the family activity is not a universally held belief. In many cultural communities, people believe it is important for the infant and caregiver to maintain close physical proximity; when the baby needs to sleep,

he or she does so while being carried about or on the body. In some cultural communities, as Hale (1983, 25) states, "socialization emphasizes the closeness of people. Physical and psychological closeness are reinforced by encouragement of body contact between people." When families immigrate to the United States, they bring the roots of their child-rearing practices from their homeland. Hale and Small both discuss the influences of the "old country" on sleeping arrangements. In countries where children are typically breast-fed for a longer period than they are in the United States and held a great deal of the time, even when they are not being breast-fed, the children also usually sleep with their mothers. Not all families have space for members to sleep alone and in separate rooms. Whatever the reason may be, a mother who is used to having her baby sleeping with her may well request that the child not be put in a crib to learn to sleep alone.

Values about sleeping and napping routines often cause a conflict when

the caregiving practices at home do not match those in the early care setting. In many programs in the United States, the policy of the child care program, the licensing requirements, or the interpretation of child care licensing regulations dictate separate sleeping arrangements for infants and toddlers. Consequently, when children come from home settings with different caregiving practices for sleeping, they experience a major inconsistency in care. The situation becomes difficult for all concerned—baby, teacher, and parents—when babies are accustomed to being held and rocked to sleep at home but in the child care setting are placed alone in a crib in a quiet, separate sleeping room. No wonder the children have difficulty falling asleep when they first come into group care.

Again, it is important to be sensitive and responsive to the needs of individual parents and babies and to be realistic about what is possible and best for the child in the child care setting. Together you and the parents will need to explore how to come to a mutually satisfying solution. With this particular issue, the licensing official may have to be included in discussions to be sure the requirements are truly appropriate to the infant's needs and consistent with the family's child-rearing practices and are not simply a culturally biased interpretation of the regulation.

Here is what happened in a program when a 15-month-old born to a refugee family arrived in the center. When the boy was placed in a crib, he screamed so loudly that his cries disturbed everyone. He just could not get used to the crib. The teachers learned that at home, which was crowded with family members, the boy never slept alone in a crib in a dark room. Over time, staff members discov-

ered that if they just let the boy stay in the play room when he got tired, he would eventually find a corner to cuddle in and go to sleep. Everything was fine until the licensing official arrived one day, pointed at the sleeping child, and asked, "What is he doing there?" The head teacher explained, but the licensing official just kept shaking her head, "No!" After a long discussion, the head teacher finally asked to see the regulation, which as it turns out stated that every child was entitled to quiet, undisturbed sleep. She pointed out that he did not get it in the crib room, and nobody else did, either. A waiver was granted, and the only stipulation was that the child had to have a clean sheet under him for sanitation reasons.

Summary

There are no "right" answers about values or the extent to which teachers should adapt their practices in any of the situations discussed in this chapter. Even practices that are considered developmentally appropriate in infant and toddler caregiving routines are influenced by cultural, professional, and personal beliefs. The practices reflect the predominant culture's beliefs and values. It is important for everyone in early care and education to be knowledgeable about both accepted caregiving practices and other child-rearing beliefs and practices, keeping in mind that in another cultural context that culture's practices would be accepted for that setting.

Diversity of beliefs and values often brings conflict. In child care, many diverse beliefs manifest themselves in different caregiving practices related to everyday, routine activities. The purpose of this guide is to help you tune in to the sensitivity required to work with someone else's baby. In this chapter, various routines and associated values and caregiving practices are highlighted to help sensitize you to the differences you will encounter regularly as a teacher. Such differences are inevitable with the increasing cultural diversity that communities experience today.

What is not necessarily inevitable is that one cultural view remains or becomes dominant over another. Instead of automatically responding in the usual way, take time to listen to parents who want something different for their babies from what is ordinarily provided. Put yourself in their shoes. Tune in. Be sensitive. Try to build a relationship with each family and increase communication. Both of those strategies will help you find out what is really behind a request—especially one that you question. Have ongoing conversations with family members about child-rearing and family practices. Understanding parents' cultural backgrounds comes only through finding out firsthand about the culture, not by labeling or stereotyping a family because it belongs to a particular group.

Be sensitive to the child's feelings. When infants and toddlers experience little continuity between home and child care, they can have a difficult time. It is important to build bridges. Provide consistency with the child-rearing at home whenever possible so that the child will feel comfortable in care outside the home. A good idea is to talk with all the families about routine caregiving and family practices as part of your enrollment and orientation procedures before the child is enrolled. By doing so, you will learn what the child is used to. The enrollment/ orientation is also the time to go to work on building relationships with each family. It may not necessarily be easy to accomplish, but is well worth the time and effort.

When you understand different values and beliefs, you will be able to collaborate with families to develop harmony between what happens at home and what happens in the program. It may not always be culturally consistent, but if you are at least as responsive as possible, the care you provide for infants and toddlers is more likely to support the culture of the home. To give that kind of support, it is necessary to come to some kind of agreement about what is best for this baby from this family in the care program even when the usual practices may need to be modified.

References

Aquino, Consuelo. 1981. "The Filipino in America." In *Culture and Childrearing,* edited by Ann L. Clark. Philadelphia: F. A. Davis.

Barrera, Isaura, Robert M. Corso, and Dianne McPherson. 2003. *Skilled Dialogue: Strategies for Responding to Cultural Diversity in Early Childhood.* Baltimore, MD: Paul H. Brookes.

Brazelton, T. Berry, and Joshua D. Sparrow. 2004a. *Feeding Your Child the Brazelton Way.* Cambridge, MA: Da Capo Press.

———. 2004b. *Toilet Training the Brazelton Way.* Cambridge, MA: Da Capo Press.

Cowee, Marion. 2012. Personal communication, May 29, 2012.

Gerber, Magda, ed. 1989. *Resources for Infant Educarers Manual.* Los Angeles: Resources for Infant Educarers.

Hale, Janice. 1983. "Black Children: Their Roots, Culture, and Learning Styles." In *Understanding the Multicultural Experience in Early Childhood Education,* edited by Olivia N. Saracho and Bernard Spodek. Washington, DC: National Association for the Education of Young Children.

Hammond, Ruth Anne. 2009. *Respecting Babies: A New look at Magda Gerber's RIE Approach.* Washington, DC: Zero to Three.

Liamputtong, Pranee, ed. 2011. *Infant Feeding Practices: A Cross-Cultural Perspective.* New York: Springer.

McKenna, James J. 2000. "Cultural Influences on Infant and Childhood Sleep Biology, and the Science That Studies It: Toward a More Inclusive Paradigm." In *Sleep and Breathing in Children: A Developmental Approach,* edited by Gerald M. Loughlin and John L. Carroll, 199–230. New York: Marcel Dekker.

Morrow, Robert D. 1987. "Cultural Differences—Be Aware!" *Academic Therapy* 23 (November): 143–49.

Rogoff, Barbara. 2011. *Developing Destinies: A Mayan Midwife and Town.* New York: Oxford University Press.

———. 2003. *The Cultural Nature of Human Development.* New York: Oxford University Press.

———. 1990. *Apprenticeship in Thinking: Cognitive Development in Social Context.* New York: Oxford University Press.

Sandoval, Mercedes C., and Maria C. De La Roza. 1986. "Cross-Cultural Perspective for Serving the Hispanic Client." In *Cross-Cultural Training for Mental Health Professionals,* edited by Harriet P. Lefley and Paul B. Pedersen. Springfield, IL: Charles C. Thomas.

Sears, William, and Martha Sears. 2003. *The Baby Book: Everything You Need to Know About Your Baby—From Birth to Age Two.* New York: Little, Brown and Company.

———. 2001. *The Attachment Parenting Book.* New York: Little, Brown and Company.

Shelov, Steven P., and Tanya Remer Altman. 2009. *Caring for Your Baby and Young Child Birth to Age 5.* 5th ed. Elk Grove Village, IL: American Academy of Pediatrics.

Small, Meredith. 1998. *Our Babies, Ourselves: How Biology and Culture Shape the Way We Parent.* New York: Anchor Books.

Sodetani-Shibata, Aimee Emiko. 1981. "The Japanese American." In *Culture and Childrearing,* edited by Ann L. Clark. Philadelphia: F. A. Davis.

Spock, Benjamin, and Robert Needlman. 2011. *Dr. Spock's Baby and Child Care.* 9th ed. New York: Pocket Books.

Wolraich, Mark. 2003. *American Academy of Pediatrics Guide to Toilet Training.* New York: Bantam Books. http://pediatrics.uchicago.edu/chiefs/ClinicCurriculum/documents/ToiletTrainingfinal.pdf (accessed March 21, 2012).

Section Three
Creating Collaborative, Reciprocal Relationships with Linguistically Diverse Families

Developing Culturally Responsive Caregiving Practices: Acknowledge, Ask, and Adapt

Louise Derman-Sparks

The best interests of children must be the primary concern in making decisions that may affect them.
—UNICEF 1990.

Culturally responsive caregiving is for *all* infants and toddlers—in all settings. It is both a conceptual and practical approach to implementing respectful and relationship-based care grounded in reciprocity between staff members and families. This chapter offers key strategies for providing culturally responsive care in any setting.

At the heart of culturally responsive care and education is partnering with families. This means recognizing families' areas of expertise, including expectations and hopes for their child, child-rearing strategies, daily life rituals, language, and other aspects of their home culture—for example, how they handle discipline (Derman-Sparks and Olsen Edwards 2010). Culturally responsive care calls for a melding between what the professional believes and knows and what the families of infant/toddlers believe and know. Therefore infant/toddler programs will differ from setting to setting, depending on the adaptations made to the particular needs and backgrounds of the children and families served. Through collaboration, everyone in the partnership benefits:

- *Infant/toddler care teachers* gain an expanded, richer, more powerful awareness of the complexities of how children develop and learn. They are better able to establish strong relationships with families because they develop a deeper understanding of the families and of themselves.

- *Family members* are better able to build trusting partnerships with the child care staff when they feel that they are respected by the staff. They are more assured that their precious infant or toddler will be safe and well cared for.

- *Children* gain a deeper sense of security, support, and predictability in their lives, conditions that are essential for emotional and cognitive development. They sense they are on an equal playing field where they can grow toward their full potential.

Thinking/Doing Activity 1, presented at the end of this chapter, will help you explore the benefits of experiencing cultural differences.

The Process of Culturally Responsive Care

Ongoing, dynamic, mutually respectful interactions among the families and staff members generate culturally responsive infant/toddler care and education. These practices are constructed in real time in response to real situations that arise in early childhood care and education programs. Culturally responsive care involves the weaving together of both professional and family practices and is therefore the opposite of "either/or" solutions to cultural differences between staff and family members or among staff.

However, a culturally responsive approach does not mean "giving up" all that you have previously learned about working with infants and toddlers. Nor does it mean that the program totally reproduces the culture of each family. By definition, group infant/toddler settings—both family- and center-based care programs—serve infants and toddlers from more than one family. The majority of early childhood programs in the United States are made up of families from numerous cultural groups. Even when families come from the same cultural group, it is unlikely that they will all apply cultural patterns in child-rearing in the same way.

Creative thinking is imperative. Some early childhood educators think of culturally responsive care as building a "third space"—one that integrates staff and family practices but is not exactly how any one staff or family member may want it to be. Instead, a "third space" is its own culture—reflecting a respectful composite of the beliefs and practices of staff and families. A culturally responsive "third space" enables you to support the healthy development of all children and their families' way of child-rearing, while also incorporating what you know as an early childhood professional.

To practice culturally responsive infant/toddler caregiving, a blend of particular skills and attitudes is needed

for working with families and colleagues to generate and use "third space" solutions. You do *not* need to know, nor can you know, everything about the cultures of all the children with whom you work. Each new situation—a new child and family, a new caregiving setting, a new staff member—will require culturally responsive strategies to gain the knowledge and develop the practices necessary for that situation. This is an ongoing learning process.

The fundamental challenge is to stay open to learning from family and staff members whose particular child-rearing beliefs and practices differ from your own. Examining your ideas and behaviors through the lens of cultural diversity may be uncomfortable. Culturally responsive care also asks you to make modifications in the way you work to best meet the needs of the children in your care.

Changing behavior can be even more challenging than self-reflection, because doing so asks you to take risks and to go beyond your comfort zone. It can make you feel self-conscious and worried about making mistakes. Characteristics such as curiosity, caring, willingness to learn and to change, and a sense of humor help make the learning process work. Your shared humanness with the people you serve is the bridge.

Four skills are needed to be a culturally responsive teacher:

Skill 1: Become aware of your cultural beliefs and values about how children develop and how best to nurture and raise them.

Skill 2: Become a critical thinker about cultural assumptions that are embedded in the thinking of the infant/toddler care and education field.

Skill 3: Use respectful strategies to discover people's cultural beliefs about child development and child-rearing. This includes learning about how other staff members and families think.

Skill 4: Use problem-solving strategies to create collaborative solutions that reflect both staff and families' child-rearing ideas and practices, and to resolve disagreements stemming from cultural differences.

The first skill emphasizes that when you do "what comes naturally," you act on your cultural assumptions about children and child-rearing, even though you may not consciously think about those assumptions. You use those assumptions to judge what is normal, what is right, or what is best. However, doing what comes naturally to you may not always be best for a particular child, because your actions may conflict with another set of beliefs and rules about child-rearing.

Most people become aware of their cultural assumptions when they experience a cultural conflict in a particular situation. However, a professional needs to learn how to regularly uncover and examine the cultural beliefs that influence how she or he works—not just when a particular cultural difference with a family is experienced. Skill 1 also requires awareness of the assumptions, stereotypes, and biases about other cultural groups that you learned while growing up, and how they influence your attitudes and behaviors. This "self-awareness work" necessitates both personal reflection and sharing with other staff members in the context of a program culture that fosters open communication.

The second skill requires thinking about what it means to be a professional. Is a professional someone who establishes reciprocal learning and problem-solving relationships? Or, is a professional someone who is a holder of knowledge and who uses this knowledge to educate clients? As previously discussed, integrating professional knowledge with knowledge learned from families is at the heart of engaging in culturally responsive caregiving. If this collaborative approach does not fit with one's idea of what it means to be a professional, one must try to identify the reasons for the incompatibility. Then new perspectives and knowledge about collaboration need to be considered. Joining in staff discussions about what it means to be an early childhood professional is part of a culturally responsive approach.

Skill 2 also requires that staff work together to critically examine professional training about infant/toddler development and best caregiving practices. This is not a question of throwing out all that was learned in higher education—or "throwing out the baby with the bath water." It does mean uncovering the cultural assumptions underlying research as well as the conclusions based on research that infant/toddler care programs draw upon to inform their practices.

Skill 3 involves finding out about the child-rearing goals, beliefs, and practices of families. Gathering this data takes place over time—not just in the first meeting with a family—and rests on building warm, respectful relationships with each family. Always keep in mind that families from the same ethnic background do not express their culture in the same way in their daily lives; some families may be very traditional, while others may reflect the practices of mainstream American culture. Furthermore, even families that have many cultural similarities may act out their cultural beliefs in different ways. In attempts to understand each child's behavior within his or her cultural context, be aware that some behaviors that deviate from your definition (or even the infant/toddler field's definition) of "normal" may not be problematic. A rule of thumb is to assume the behavior is normal development until more information is gathered.

Families' ease in relating their child-rearing hopes, beliefs, and practices to program staff will vary. Some families will plunge right in, others will share bit by bit, and some will need time to build a trusting relationship with teachers before disclosing their child-rearing beliefs. Some families will find it easy to raise concerns, while others will not even consider raising concerns or challenging a school policy. Responsibility for opening up and sustaining genuine conversations lies with the professional. It is the professional's job to listen and learn as well as to talk and to initiate the search for common ground and solutions to specific differences. It is helpful to remember that for many people, *family* consists not only of parents, but also other family members such as grandparents, aunts and uncles, and the like.

Skill 4 is the ability to modify and add to how one works with infants/toddlers

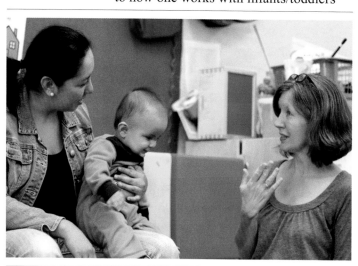

and their families. This component uses the previous three skills. It is the essential step in building a culturally responsive program. Practice is necessary for these four basic skills to become a regular, natural way to work with infants/toddlers. Teachers will also grow more readily in these four skills if the program leader creates a culture that supports learning how to provide culturally responsive care and education.

See Thinking/Doing Activities 2 and 3 at the end of this chapter.

Acknowledge, Ask, and Adapt

This section explores a way of working that will enable professionals to create culturally responsive caregiving practices that are mutually satisfying to staff and the families with whom they work. It will foster the growth of *all* the children in the care program. This approach involves three strategic steps called "Acknowledge, Ask, and Adapt." Learning to use this approach takes time and patience. Teachers will always have something new to learn about themselves, their colleagues, and the families.

Acknowledge

This first step is an act of recognition that cultural differences are real and meaningful—and need further investigation when a specific issue arises with a child or family or between a teacher and another staff member. It also uses one's growing awareness that the cultural ideas embedded in early childhood professional concepts do not necessarily fit all cultural child-rearing beliefs and behaviors. The Acknowledge step requires staying calm with the dynamics of cultural diversity, remembering that cultural differences do not always lead to a conflict. In most cases, teachers will be able to figure out a working solution. Some differences will be easily incorporated in practice; some will require more involved problem solving.

The Acknowledge step involves becoming aware that cultural differences or conflicts are not abstract; they arise in specific situations. The scenarios later in this chapter offer a few examples of such differences. Indicators of a potential cultural difference or conflict might be a family member's upset or confused reaction to an interaction between the teacher and his or her child; a child's response of discomfort, confusion, or anxiety; or from information gathered from a family member or another teacher about the cultural child-rearing practices of the child's family. A potential cultural issue may also arise when a family disagrees with a concern raised about a particular behavior of their infant or toddler.

The Acknowledge step consists of the following actions:

- *Admit that a cultural difference or conflict may exist* on a particular aspect of caregiving in a certain situation. Check your feelings—and take the time to address responses such as discomfort, annoyance, or frustration. Avoid making a quick judgment that the family's way must be the problem.

- *Let the family member(s) know that there is an issue to discuss* and set up a place and time for a conversation. Show respect for the family through a caring manner—and in the willingness to meet at a time and place that works for the family. Be sensitive to language issues—such as the need for an interpreter—with a family who is not fluent in English.

- *Uncover and acknowledge the specific cultural beliefs* that influence your view of the situation. Sort out your

feelings about the situation as well. If teachers understand their own reactions to the specific situation, the more effective they will be in talking with the family.

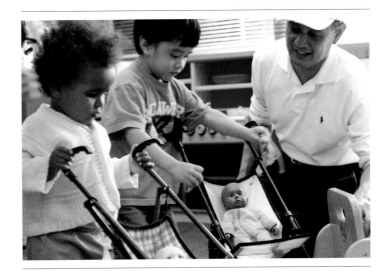

Ask

The second step is to gather data. It includes finding out about the family's specific cultural beliefs and values and identifying the developmental issues and best practices regarding the situation under consideration. Do not rush the Ask step. The goal is to get the information necessary to eventually do collaborative problem solving. The Ask step consists of the following actions:

Find out how the family members view the issue and how they would handle the caregiving situation. Ask questions and watch the interactions between the child and family member in the child care setting and, if possible, interactions at the child's home. A variety of questions may be needed to get the information. Be careful not to enter into the conversation with assumptions about the family's socialization beliefs based on the cultural patterns of a particular ethnic group. Listen attentively to the specific beliefs and behaviors of the family. Avoid approaching the family in ways that may put them on the defensive.

Take time to reflect on information gained from a conversation with the family. Feelings about the family member's viewpoint and practice should be examined. One may be comfortable with adapting to it. On the other hand, teachers may be uncomfortable because the family's viewpoint is contrary to basic cultural beliefs about caregiving. Or a teacher may think it contradicts what the field of infant/toddler care believes about development and best practices, or that it does not conform to licensing regulations. Teachers may need to talk with other staff or the program leader about these feelings and what to do before moving on to the Adapt step. It may be necessary to have more conversations with the family to better understand the issue under consideration.

Adapt

The third and last problem-solving step is to use the information gathered in the Acknowledge and Ask steps about oneself, the family, and the early childhood education field. The goal is always to find the most effective way to support each child's best growth, taking into account the cultural issues.

a. Invite collaborative problem solving. Take the initiative to ask the family to join you in figuring out the best way to work with their child on the issue under consideration. Make sure that both the family and you are clear about the specific details of the matter. Assure the family that the goal is to figure out a mutually satisfying solution that will be in their child's best interests.

b. *Facilitate a discussion that allows both family members and you to suggest various ideas and explore their strengths and weaknesses.* Look for the points of commonality. Some families may find it hard to engage in this kind of collaborative problem solving with teachers since they are not familiar with being in a partnership with a professional. Be patient, keep the conversation from having an adversarial tone, and do not give up. The time spent together will be well worth it.

c. *Come to a mutual decision.* The objective of this step is to reach agreement on the best-for-the-child action in the situation. Flexibility and creativity are essential throughout this process. Several outcomes are possible: (1) the teacher understands and agrees to follow the solution preferred by the family member to maintain consistency with the family's child-rearing beliefs; (2) the family and teacher agree to an action that is a modification of what *each of them does;* or (3) the family, upon understanding why a teacher uses a particular practice, approves the practice or decides to live with it. Sometimes, even with sensitive use of the Acknowledge, Ask, and Adapt steps, it may not be possible to find a mutual agreement on a particular cultural conflict. Legal regulations for the program may interfere with finding a solution that is satisfactory to the family. In this case, be sure there is no way to find a compromise. Even when a family's request conflicts with a licensing regulation, it may be possible to find a solution that will satisfy the regulations and meet at least some of the family's needs. Another possible barrier to finding a mutually agreeable solution is when a teacher's convictions about an issue do not allow for any modifications in practice. When that is the case, much soul searching about one's beliefs is needed and the family must be sensitively informed why no changes will be made.

If the process of communication and negotiation has been conducted with care and respect, even when a cultural difference cannot be satisfactorily resolved, the family will at least know that a sincere attempt was made. However, a family may decide to place their child in another child care setting that will be more culturally consistent for them. In such a case it may be best, in collaboration with the

program director, to bring in a consultant who specializes in culturally responsive, anti-bias care and education to explore ways to handle similar cultural conflicts in the future.

Identifying Culturally Responsive and Culturally Insensitive Practices

The following scenarios of typical caregiving situations that have occurred in child care settings illustrate the Acknowledge, Ask, and Adapt steps in action. After each scenario, three variations are described of how the teacher in each scenario handled the situation and then rated as to effectiveness. See whether you agree or disagree with those ratings. Think about how you might use the three steps to address each scenario and how you would rate your actions.

Scenario 1: A Baby Crying

Here are three variations of how Joan, the infant care teacher, might respond to a baby who is crying.

The Scenario

Rosy, six months old, is waking up from her nap and begins to cry. Joan, her teacher, has begun to dress Mark. She lets Rosy cry while she finishes dressing Mark (which takes about five minutes), then picks Rosy up. In the meantime, Rosy's mother (Mrs. H) has come early to pick up her daughter and sees the incident. When Joan greets her, Mrs. H takes Rosy from her and holds Rosy tightly. Rosy does not come to child care the next two days. When Joan calls to find out what has happened, Mrs. H says that Rosy will be back the next day, but she does not return until the following Monday. By then, Joan is concerned. On the day Rosy returns, Joan takes Mrs. H aside and asks why Rosy was out so long. Mrs. H replies, "Rosy was upset. You didn't take good care of her."

Response X

Joan is surprised and hurt. She feels she has taken good care of Rosy. She replies: "I take good care of all my babies. I would never do anything to hurt Rosy." Mrs. H: "Last time, you let her cry too much." Joan thinks back to Rosy's last day: "I was dressing Mark. I let Rosy cry only a few minutes. " Mrs. H: "You waited too long." Joan, a little annoyed: "No, I didn't. I had to take care of Mark first. Besides, it doesn't hurt a baby to cry a little." Mrs. H insists: "That's not good. In my country, we always pick up the baby right away."

By now Joan is really annoyed: "Mrs. H, in this country we do not believe in spoiling babies. It's good for Rosy to learn that an adult won't always come immediately when she cries." Mrs. H looks upset but does not say any more.

Joan decides that she has to do something at the center to ensure that Rosy does not become spoiled. She starts to let Rosy cry a little longer before she goes to her so that Rosy can learn to wait. Rosy begins to cry more often when her mother leaves her in the morning. Joan sees that as evidence of Mrs. H's "overprotection" and continues with her plan of teaching Rosy to wait. Rosy is not doing as well, so Joan decides to speak with Mrs. H again to find out what is going wrong at home.

Rating of Response X: This handling of the baby crying situation is culturally insensitive. It does not show awareness or concern about the cultural issues in the scenario or any openness by the teacher in terms of modifying her actions.

Acknowledge gets a minus. Joan pays attention only to her own feelings and acts defensively by trying to justify herself. Joan does not acknowledge either Rosy's mother's concern or the need for solving the problem.

Ask gets a minus. Joan does not try to find out anything about what is behind Mrs. H's concern. Nor does she show any evidence of recognizing that her own cultural assumptions are only one way of thinking about the issue. Instead, she makes a quick judgment that Mrs. H must be spoiling Rosy.

Adapt gets a minus. Joan makes no effort to adapt her behavior to Rosy's family's cultural beliefs and behaviors and makes things worse for Rosy by creating an even wider gap between what Rosy's family does at home and what she, Joan, does to avoid spoiling Rosy. When Rosy shows signs of not thriving at the center, Joan again assumes the cause must be a problem at home. Joan does not use good communication, negotiation, or conflict-resolution skills.

Response Y

Joan is surprised and concerned. She thought that Rosy's mother trusted her. Joan: "Mrs. H, I'm sorry you feel that way. I care very much about Rosy and do not want to hurt her in any way." Mrs. H: "Last time you let her cry too long." Joan: "I had to finish dressing Mark, and she didn't sound too upset. I was going to pick her up shortly." Mrs. H: "That's too long. That's not good for babies." Joan: "What do you do at home when Rosy starts to cry?" Mrs. H: "In my house, we pick her up right away. That is good for babies."

Joan: "Well, that may work for you at home, but in child care we can't always do that. There are other babies who need care also. It won't hurt Rosy to cry a few minutes. In fact, it will be good for her. You don't want her to be spoiled." Mrs. H shakes her head: "In my country, we do not think that is good for babies." By now Joan is unhappy. She does not like having a disagreement with a family member, but she does not want to give in. Joan: "At home you can pick her up as you think best, but in child care sometimes she will have to wait."

When Joan notices that Mrs. H has become more distant and that Rosy cries more often when her mother leaves her, she begins to think that Rosy is confused by being handled one way at home and another way in child care. She decides to work with Mrs. H to convince her to let Rosy cry a little longer at home before picking her up.

Rating of Response Y: This variation is partially sensitive. It shows culturally responsive behavior in steps 1 (Acknowledge) and 2 (Ask) but culturally insensitive behavior when it comes to taking action.

Acknowledge gets a plus. Joan recognizes that Rosy's mother is upset and expresses concern about how she feels.

Ask gets a plus for one part, a minus for another part. Joan gets a plus for asking for some information and for realizing that Rosy's mother's belief about how to handle crying differs from her own. She gets a minus because she moves too quickly to a solution—she does not get sufficient information from Mrs. H to determine the seriousness of the difference.

Adapt gets a minus. Joan is not willing to change her behavior at all in the child care setting. She considers it giving in rather than as adapting. When Rosy is not doing well in child care, Joan thinks Mrs. H should change how she handles crying at home. Joan does not think about how her own behavior might have made Mrs. H uneasy and may be making Rosy feel more insecure in the child care program. Because Joan does not use step 3, the consequence of response Y is culturally insensitive, even though Joan followed the first two steps.

Response Z

Joan realizes immediately that this is a serious issue. Rosy's mother has never disagreed with or criticized the teachers before. Joan: "Mrs. H, I care very much for Rosy and do not want to hurt her in any way. Please tell me what I did that you think wasn't good for her." Mrs. H: "You let her cry too long last time she was here." Joan: "When I was dressing Mark?" Mrs. H nods her head yes. Joan: "What would you have done?" Mrs. H: "I would have picked her up right away." Joan: "Sounds as though picking up a crying baby right away is very important to you." Mrs. H: "In my country, we think a mother who lets her baby cry is not good." Joan: "So when I didn't pick Rosy up right away, it worried you." Mrs. H nods again: "Yes, Rosy will be frightened." Joan: "Is that why you kept her home the past few days?" Mrs. H: "I wanted her home with me. But now I have to go back to work."

Joan: "I know it is hard for you to leave Rosy here all day, especially if you think I was doing something that would upset her. I did not know that what seemed to me like letting Rosy cry only a little while seemed too long to you. Now that I understand how you feel and what you do, I will be more careful about picking her up as soon as she cries. Will that make you feel safer leaving her here?" Mrs. H smiles: "Yes."

Joan: "I also need to tell you that because other babies need attention in child care, and sometimes there is only one adult free, once in a while Rosy may have to wait a little to be picked up. That might happen if another baby is in physical danger or is hurt and I am the only adult available. Will you be comfortable with that?" Mrs. H: "I know there are other babies. I just want to know that Rosy will be safe."

Joan: "I'm so glad you let me know that you were unhappy with what I did. Please be sure to let me know if anything else I do bothers you. That way we will make sure that Rosy gets the best care I can give her." Mrs. H: "You tell me also if there is something I need to know."

After the conversation with Rosy's mother, Joan realizes she has not thought much about what the family members of her other babies, who come from a number of different cultural groups, think about how to handle crying. She also wonders if other mothers from the same cultural background as Mrs. H feel the same way as Mrs. H. She decides to ask each family about their views when they pick up their babies during the following week. She also decides that a newsletter about different families' ideas about handling crying and a family members meeting might help family members understand that different children may need different kinds of responses for them to feel secure in child care.

Rating of Response Z: This approach to the crying baby scenario is culturally responsive. The teacher pays close attention to the cultural issues at each step and demonstrates willingness to make changes.

Acknowledge gets a plus. Joan immediately makes clear that she is open to hearing about what upset Rosy's mother. She also responds to Mrs. H's feelings. Joan shows that she is not defensive about making mistakes; instead, she accepts that she does and wants to learn more so that she can do better.

Ask gets a plus. Joan asks questions that help get her the kind of information she needs to understand why Mrs. H is upset (Joan learns not only how Mrs. H handles crying but also that her definition of being a good mother depends on her response).

Adapt gets a plus. Joan is willing to modify her behavior to be more consistent with Mrs. H's behavior. She does that for Rosy's sake (so Rosy will feel secure), for Mrs. H's sake (so Mrs. H will feel secure leaving Rosy at child care), and for her own sake (so she will continue a trusting relationship with Mrs. H). Mrs. H also has to do a little adapting because Joan lets her know that once in a while she may not be able to pick Rosy up immediately when she cries. Joan also recognizes that she needs more information from the rest of the family members and makes a plan for getting it. That behavior indicates that Joan is not defensive about not knowing everything; instead, she is comfortable in planning how to get the information she needs when she discovers that she needs it.

See Thinking/Doing Activity 4 at the end of this chapter.

Scenario 2: Babies Wearing Protective Amulets

Five staff members in an infant/toddler center try to decide what to do about a cultural practice of some families that conflicts with one of the regulations at the center. Each staff member represents one kind of response to the problem. As you read their discussion, think about which solutions you consider culturally insensitive and which ones are culturally responsive. Which solution would you choose? Or would you create a solution different from those mentioned?

The Scenario

Some of the families in the center come from an ethnic group whose cultural practice is to have babies wear a protective amulet around the neck. The amulets have an important religious significance; the families believe the amulets protect their babies against illnesses and other dangers. However, the child care center regulation states that infants and toddlers may not wear necklaces for safety reasons. Injuries may be caused by other babies pulling the necklaces too tight or yanking them off or by the babies chewing on them and choking. The amulets might also be lost.

Staff Discussion

Rosa:	I think we have a real problem here. I asked Mrs. M about the amulet, and she said she never takes it off. The baby could come to harm if she did.
Harriet:	Boy, what superstition. I don't think we should give in to it. It's very simple—wearing a necklace is against the regulations. Besides, we know that taking off the amulet will not hurt the baby.
Mark:	We may not think it will; but if the families think so, they will be very unhappy and anxious if we remove the amulets.
Lynn:	Well, I don't see what else we can do. I mean, I feel sympathy for the families' feelings, but we cannot let the kids wear them—it's too dangerous.
Rosa:	I agree that it could be dangerous, but I don't think we can just ask the families to take them off.
Harriet:	Well, I think we are making a big deal out of nothing. Families have to accept the rules when they use the center. Besides, I don't think we should be encouraging such practices. They are living in America now.
Rosa:	They are not your religious beliefs, but they are the families' beliefs. They are as important to them as yours are to you.
Lynn:	Let's just tell them we are sorry, but it is not safe and it is against the rules. We can say their children can wear the amulets at home and reassure them that we have other ways to keep the babies safe and healthy at the center.
Mark:	I think we need to do more. We have to consider the children's safety from both our point of view and the families' point of view.
Harriet:	If we don't follow the regulations, we will be out of compliance.
Rosa:	We need to find solutions that deal with the regulations and also meet the families' needs. I can think of one. I am sure we can think of others. I suggest that we ask family members to take off the amulets when they come to the center and put them in a special box that we will keep on a shelf in the room. When their child goes home, they can put the amulet back on.
Mark:	I think we need to ask the families if that will be enough. If it isn't, we need other ideas. What if we suggest pinning the amulet to the underside of the child's shirt so that it is still on the child but cannot be pulled?
Rosa:	We might also suggest that the baby can wear the amulet if it fits securely around the neck—not too tight and not loose enough to be pulled.
Lynn:	That last suggestion would be going against the regulations.
Mark:	I think we sometimes have to consider modifying regulations to meet families' needs. If the family members don't feel that their child is safe, we will not be able to build a trusting relationship with them, even if we know our regulation is intended for the children's safety.
Harriet:	I will not agree to a solution that goes against the regulation.

Rosa: I think we first need to talk with the families before we decide among ourselves which solution to use. They may have other ideas of their own. I think we can find a solution that fits the intent of the regulation.

Mark: In raising this issue with family members, I suggest we do three things: one, explain our safety concerns to the families—how, in the center, where many babies and toddlers are playing with each other, necklaces like the amulets can cause injuries. We should explain what those injuries could be and how accidents can happen quickly, even when adults, who may be attending to other babies or toddlers, are around. Two, we should ask more about the importance of the amulets and assure the family members that we empathize with their viewpoint. Three, we should suggest some of the possible options and find out what other ideas they have. Then, together, we can figure out what solutions will be acceptable to them and to us.

Rosa and Mark volunteer to meet with the five families and report back to the rest of the staff.

Rating the Staff Members' Responses

Harriet's response is culturally insensitive. She does not use any steps of the culturally responsive process. She refuses to acknowledge that there is a problem, she does not even consider asking the family members about their beliefs, and, she is not willing to consider any solution except to remove the amulets.

Lynn's response shows some cultural sensitivity in the Acknowledge step but shows cultural insensitivity in the other steps. She acknowledges a problem and expresses more feeling for the families than Harriet does. However, she is not interested in learning about the family members' beliefs and is not willing to make any changes to meet their needs. She sees the safety of the children only from the center's perspective.

Mark and Rosa are culturally responsive in their approach to resolving the situation. They know how to use the Acknowledge, Ask, and Adapt steps to work on creating a mutually satisfying solution. They want to communicate and work with the family members to find a strategy that respects the families' beliefs and also meets the safety requirements of the center. Mark is more willing than Rosa to modify the regulations, if necessary.

See Thinking/Doing Activity 5 at the end of this chapter to examine your responses to this kind of situation.

Scenario 3: Babies Staying Clean or Engaging in Active Learning

In this scenario, a cultural belief of several families conflicts with the teacher's pedagogical principles.

The Scenario

Several families in the center strongly believe that by keeping toddlers clean and neat during the day, teachers demonstrate care and the instruction of healthy behavior. At home, whenever the toddlers get messy or dirty, an adult immediately cleans them. In contrast with that view, the teacher believes that an essential part of children's healthy development is for children to participate actively with materials such as sand, water, and paint, to feed themselves, and so forth—which means that toddlers will get messy. She also believes that toddlers should help clean themselves. The teacher does help them clean up at times during the day (after an activity is over, before eating, and before a nap); but if she cleaned every child as soon as he or she got messy, the teacher would be spending most of her time cleaning up. She does not think that is necessary.

Handling the "Babies Staying Clean" Scenario

How do you think the teacher should handle the situation? Jot down your ideas for each step.

Acknowledge

What could the teacher say to herself and to the family members to communicate her awareness that this is a problem that they need to solve jointly?

Ask

What questions could the teacher ask the family members to get information that will help her understand more precisely the family members' concerns and what they think is an appropriate practice?

Adapt

How can the teacher open a negotiation with the family members about what to do? The teacher does not want to stop children from being active with materials or stop them from learning how to take care of themselves. How can the teacher explain why she allows children to get messy without immediately cleaning them and also communicate that she wants to find ways to meet the family members' needs? What modifications of child care practice might the teacher explore with the family members? What is fair to expect family members to accept as modification of their home behaviors while their children are at the center?

Rating Yourself

Now, look over your notes as you consider the following questions for each step.

Acknowledge

- Have you examined your thoughts and feelings about the issue?

- Are you willing to explore the issue with the family with an open mind, or are you assuming before you talk with them that the family's request about cleanliness will interfere with your program or with their toddler's development?

- How will you communicate to the family that you want to find a mutually satisfying solution that takes into account their cultural perspective? (Remember, if you merely state the program policy without exploring the issue with an open mind, you are not using a culturally responsive approach.)

Ask

- Will the types of questions you asked give you the information you need to understand why family members think it is important for their toddler to stay clean at all times? Do your questions and tone communicate openness and support so that family members will feel comfortable telling you what they really think?

Adapt

- Have you clarified the situation in a way that invites family members to figure out with you how their child can participate in a full range of activities?

- Have you shown openness to finding a way to meet the family members' needs for cleanliness and neatness while also honoring your educational beliefs? For example, you might decide to add more opportunities during the day in which you help the toddler get clean. If you are in a center, you might get a washing machine so that clothes that are especially dirty can be washed before the children go home. (These are only examples, not necessarily what you would do.)

Scenario 4: "Two Mommies"

This scenario involves an openly lesbian couple who enrolled their child in an infant/toddler care program. It focuses on differences of beliefs and attitudes among staff members concerning the definition of a legitimate family unit. It opens up the thorny issue of a teacher judging a family as engaging in "wrong" or unacceptable behavior because that behavior contradicts the teacher's personal beliefs. What do you think is the responsibility of a culturally responsive professional in such a situation?

The Scenario

For the first time, a family consisting of two female parents—both of whom are open about being lesbians—joins the infant/toddler care center. During the intake session, both women make it clear that they want to be acknowledged as the parents of the infant. They cross out "father" on the admission form and substitute "mother," so that there is a place for each woman to write down her name. They also ask permission to contribute a poster that shows "two-mommy families" and a few picture books with images of two-mommy and two-daddy families. The center director consents to their requests. However, when she informs the staff about the family, conflicting responses to having openly lesbian parents in the program necessitates a staff discussion.

Christine, the teacher in whose room the infant will be placed, is uncomfortable with the situation. She tells other staff members that she thinks it is wrong to encourage homosexuality, since she believes it is a sin. She wants the director to tell the family that only one parent can be considered the infant's mother, and that person is the only family member who should interact with the program. She also refuses to use the poster or picture books the family wants to contribute.

Marie, an assistant teacher, agrees with Christine. She even suggests that, to avoid problems, the director not admit the family into the program. She explains that since homosexuals cannot properly raise a child, she does not think the program should encourage homosexuality by accepting the infant.

Rachel explains that she has no problem with a two-mommy family, but she is worried that admitting this family into the program will cause problems with other families. In the interests of keeping the peace, she reluctantly supports Christine's suggestion to identify only one person as the infant's mother and that no materials show two-mommy families.

Carrie disagrees with the others. She takes the position that, as professionals, they have a responsibility to support all families equally and to make sure that all the infants and toddlers have their family visible in the program. She reminds her colleagues that the family composition and members' roles within families vary widely. Carrie further explains that she is not questioning her colleagues' personal beliefs, but argues that professionals need to act according to professional ethics and not just according to their personal beliefs.

Sarah agrees with Carrie. She reminds her colleagues of the following excerpt from the *California Early Childhood*

Educator Competencies publication: "Cultural perspectives of children, families, staff, and colleagues vary widely on issues such as differences in individual children's learning, strengths, and abilities; gender identity and gender-specific roles; family composition and member roles" (CDE 2011, 21). Sarah reminds staff that there was a time when many people considered all single mothers to be immoral and bad parents. Sarah further states that it is equally prejudicial to automatically assume that all two-mommy families are "bad." Carrie adds to Sarah's point, declaring that child-rearing problems arise in families of all kinds of cultural backgrounds and configurations.

Rating the Staff Responses

This scenario addresses a current topic in early childhood care and education programs. How might the cultural responsiveness rating criteria be applied? Some would argue that this scenario is not about cultural responsiveness because it is about religious, personal, and moral beliefs. However, religious and personal moral beliefs are also cultural. In addition, this scenario raises the uncomfortable issue of defining prejudice in teacher responses to an aspect of human diversity with which they disagree. For instance, not so long ago, some people argued that interracial families and biracial children were unnatural and wrong, often invoking religious reasons to justify their position. But in modern times, interracial families and biracial children are a growing and accepted part of society.

Following is *one* way to rate the degree of cultural responsiveness of the staff members in the scenario. Would you rate them differently or similarly? Why?

Christine and Marie's responses are not culturally responsive. Asking the family to choose only one mother as the legitimate parent denies the other mother her parenting rights, thus undercutting the family. It would also make their infant's family invisible in the center. Their positions raise serious questions about whether they could truly support the infant and how they could work with the family.

Rachel's response is only partially acceptable. She acknowledges the family's right to define itself on its own terms, but she does not want to "rock the boat" by actually supporting the family. Consequently, even though her reasons differ from those of Christine and Marie, the impact on the family is still the same. She also assumes that all the other center families will agree with Christine and Marie, without giving the families a chance to speak for themselves on this issue. Avoiding potential differences among families does not create a culturally responsive culture in the center. Conversely, providing ways for families to talk with each other and staff about all issues and how they can help build a culturally responsive program for everyone is consistent with the principle of equitably supporting all families.

Sarah and Carrie are culturally responsive in their approach to handling the situation. They accept that all families have a right to be who they are and to be recognized in an infant/toddler care program. They also recognize that child-rearing problems are not connected to specific ways of life in themselves, but may exist in families of all kinds and cultures.

Have you been part of a conversation with staff that is similar to this one? If so, what would you want to say?

In this scenario, the staff members are the ones who need to address the differences of beliefs among themselves. They can also use the Acknowledge, Ask, and Adapt steps to do this.

See Thinking/Doing Activity 6 at the end of this chapter.

Developmental Issues or Cultural Differences?

When infant/toddler care teachers are not sensitive to or choose to disregard cultural differences, they may too quickly interpret a baby's or a toddler's healthy behavior as a developmental problem. A third possibility sometimes arises: a cultural difference between what a family accepts as normal behavior and what a child needs to be able to do in the group-care setting and education program (e.g., toilet learning, eating independently). Therefore, another important part of culturally responsive caregiving is being able to identify when a behavior is a culturally different way of exhibiting normal development and when it is a developmental problem that really needs attention. Figuring out which it is entails working with the family and other staff. Chapter 3 provides teachers with specific skills and strategies to work with families to identify those child behaviors that need

special attention in a culturally responsive approach.

Generally, a specific behavior of a child will qualify as a developmental problem when it is seen as a problem in the child's culture as well. However, in some situations, the child's behavior may actually be a developmental problem that the family is not willing to acknowledge—for either cultural or personal reasons. Keep in mind that this is a response that a family (part of any cultural group) might have. Sensitively use the Acknowledge, Ask, and Adapt steps to determine whether with the conflict involves a cultural difference or a developmental issue.

It is not always easy to figure out whether a behavior is (1) culturally different but still normal, (2) a developmental problem, or (3) or the infant/toddler's response to the different culture of the group care program. Even so, it is important to take the time to do so. Prematurely identifying a child with a potential developmental problem prior to having all of the information or a delay in addressing what needs to be done may be harmful.

Determining the Nature of the Behavior

Acknowledge

1. Identify the specific concerns about the child's behavior and the reasons. Be specific. Consider what, in your own cultural background or professional training, may contribute to your uneasiness about the behavior.

2. Talk to other staff in the center or to the director, or with other family child care providers to explore if the behavior concerns them too. Talking with specialists in infant/toddler and child development who have a

culturally responsive perspective will be helpful in some cases.

3. If others agree that the behavior in question might be a developmental problem, proceed to the Ask step.

Ask

1. Respectfully communicate with the child's family members about the behavior that poses a concern, and ask for their help in understanding what the behavior means. Ask family members whether they see the same behavior at home and, if they do, what they think about it. Keep in mind that the family is a key source of information in the effort to understand the relationship between the child's home culture and his or her developmental progress.

2. If family members express no concern about the behavior, ask questions that help in understanding why it does not concern them. Keep in mind that the same behavior may be considered appropriate or expected in one cultural context and signal a problem in another. For example, a two-year-old who expects to be fed by an adult may be showing culturally appropriate behavior in one family and be considered too dependent in another. If the family members say the behavior worries them too, ask questions that help reveal why it worries them and what they think is causing the problem.

Work Toward a Solution (Adapt)

What is done after all the information is collected depends on whether it is determined that the child's behavior reflects a cultural difference or indicates a developmental issue. If the behavior reflects a cultural difference, no further

action may be needed, or a mutually agreeable way may be found to handle the behavior under consideration in the group setting of the infant/toddler program. If a teacher, after working through the Acknowledge and Ask steps, comes to the conclusion that the behavior under consideration does point to a developmental issue, it is best to work with the child's family members, other staff in the program who directly care for the child, and specialists (if necessary). The goal is to determine the causes of the problem and to create an individualized plan for working with the child in the care program, with support from the family members. Refer to chapter 3 for strategies on working with families that have young children with special needs.

Conclusion

The suggestions in this guide for practicing culturally responsive caregiving may seem overwhelming—especially if they are a new way of working for you. It is not easy to question previous learning or to change the way one is used to acting. However, the Acknowledge, Ask, and Adapt steps will become easier and often less time-consuming as they become habitual practice.

The time and energy put into becoming a more culturally responsive teacher will be worth it. Professional competence and effectiveness will be deepened. Each teacher will also grow as a human being because he or she will gain a deeper understanding of himself or herself as well as of the wide range of ways in which human beings live.

References

California Department of Education (CDE). 2011. *California Early Childhood Educator Competencies.* Sacramento: CDE.

Derman-Sparks, Louise, and Julie Olsen Edwards. 2010. *Anti-Bias Education for Young Children and Ourselves.* Washington, DC: National Association for the Education of Young Children.

National Association for Family Child Care. 2007. *NAFCC's Vision for Family Child Care.* http://www.nafcc.org.

UNICEF. 1990. "Fact Sheet: A Summary of the Rights under the Convention on the Rights of the Child." New York: UN General Assembly. http://www.unicef.org/crc/files/Rights_overview.pdf (accessed March 20, 2013).

Remind yourself of an experience you enjoyed that involved a cultural difference between you and another person.

1. Describe the experience here.

2. What do you feel you gained?

3. Why was it enjoyable?

Now, remind yourself of an experience involving a cultural difference between you and another person that you did not enjoy. Respond to questions 1 and 2 above, and then write down why the experience was not enjoyable.

Share your experiences with another staff member.

What strengths do you bring to developing culturally responsive caregiving practices?

Check the ones you feel you already have:

☐ Curiosity about others

☐ Enjoyment of others

☐ Willingness to learn from mistakes

☐ Willingness to take risks

☐ Sense of humor

☐ Creativity

☐ Flexibility

☐ Commitment

Add other strengths that you believe are important.

Now, consider your beliefs and practices about infant/toddler care and education. Which ones might be easier for you to change in order to adapt to a cultural belief or practice of the families with whom you work? Which ones would be difficult or even impossible for you to modify? Why?

Thinking/Doing Activity 3

Learning to be more culturally responsive can be challenging. What aspects of this learning process make you feel uncomfortable?

What is the worst thing you can imagine might happen?

What do you like about learning to be more culturally responsive?

Discuss with other teachers your responses to these questions.

Write down your thoughts and feelings about the ratings of the teachers for the four scenarios in this chapter. Try to be specific, and consider what might underlie your responses.

For Scenario 1 (A Baby Crying), discuss responses X, Y, and Z with other teachers who have completed the writing activity. Discuss each person's feelings about the ratings of the three responses.

Thinking/Doing Activity 5

This activity can be done with scenarios 1, 2, 3, and 4. Begin this activity by reading one of the scenarios.

Has your center or family child care home faced a similar problem?

If so, what did you do?

Would you still solve the problem in the same way?

If the situation were to arise in the future, which solution would feel most comfortable to you?

Thinking/Doing Activity 6

Write down three specific examples of cultural differences that have occurred in your infant/toddler program. How were these handled? Would you handle any of these situations differently now? If yes, how?

Use your examples and others to role-play ways to handle them; then analyze which strategies reflected cultural insensitivity and which were culturally responsive.

CHAPTER 7

Creating Collaborative, Reciprocal Relationships with Linguistically Diverse Families

Gisela Jia and Alison Wishard Guerra

In early care settings, young infants and toddlers whose home language is not English face the expected challenge of developing new routines and relationships. They also face the additional task of learning to navigate these relationships and routines through a new language. To help children with these challenges, infant/toddler care teachers can use a range of strategies. This chapter presents strategies for building trusting relationships with children and families who speak a language other than English.

To use the strategies effectively requires an understanding of the unique child-rearing values, goals, and practices of families from diverse cultural and linguistic backgrounds. Such an understanding will help teachers appreciate children's experiences and routines at home. Teachers can use such an appreciation to guide themselves through the working process of a productive, collaborative relationship. Toward this end, this chapter will briefly discuss the linguistic and communicative experiences that children bring to the early care setting, family goals and values related to language and communication, and recommended strategies for engaging in collaborative relationships with families.

Linguistic and Cultural Diversity at Home

Among children with a home language other than English, the amount of exposure to both their home language and English varies tremendously. Children who are predominantly exposed to their non-English home language(s) for the first three years of life and then begin to learn English when they enter a care setting where English is the dominant language are referred to as successive or sequential dual-language learners. Although these children may be exposed to some English through TV, older siblings, or some contacts in the community, the exposure usually is not enough for them to develop the ability to speak English. When children's main exposure to English occurs after age three, their home language foundation is already solid (Hammer, Jia, and Uchikoshi 2011), and thus they learn two languages at different times.

Another group of children, called simultaneous dual-language learners, have more early exposure to English than successive/sequential dual-language learners. For example, two parents may each speak a mixture of a shared home language and English, such as Spanish and English or Chinese and English. In another family, one parent may speak only the home language and the other parent may speak only English. And in yet another family, both parents may speak only in English while one or more additional caregivers (such as grandparents or a nanny) speak the parents' native language. Although the relative amounts of exposure to the home language and

English still vary among these children, they have adequate exposure to both English and the home language(s) such that they are able to learn two languages simultaneously prior to age three (Hoff et al. 2011). Depending on the family context for learning language, each family has different perspectives on their children's bilingual development.

Family Beliefs and Goals for Children's Bicultural and Bilingual Development

Just as families may vary in their socialization goals for their children, they are also likely to have different beliefs and goals for their children's bicultural and bilingual development that influence parenting practices. For example, almost all immigrant families believe that becoming proficient in English and becoming assimilated into or having knowledge of mainstream American culture is essential to their children's future success. However, variation occurs with each family's beliefs and goals for their children's learning and maintenance of their home language and culture. Some see home language and culture as competing for their children's resources such as time and cognitive ability, and therefore believe that "only if they abandon their language and culture will their children succeed in American society" (Garcia 1991, 6). These parents may minimize use of their home language and home cultural practices and maximize use of English both at home and in the group care setting.

Some others believe that their children staying close to their cultural roots and maintaining their home language will lead to optimal developmental outcomes. Such parents tend to maximize home language use and maintain traditional cultural practices at home and hope that home language development can be reinforced in the early care setting, particularly prior to kindergarten. Another group of parents may believe that home is where children will learn and maintain their home language, and school is where they will learn English. These parents may expect infant/toddler care teachers to speak English to their children or at least not push for their home language to be present in the group care environment.

Although some parents are clear about their beliefs about which language should be spoken where, many families feel conflicted about language and culture. There may be elements of the culture in the United States that they are eager for their children to embrace and some that they want children to avoid. In the same way, there may be elements of their home culture that they want their children to maintain and some that they permit to

give up. Such conflicts may lead to confusion in linguistic and cultural behaviors in some families but also provide an opportunity for learning. Many families are ready to absorb new information and may come to a new understanding of the role of language and culture through discussions with their early care teachers.

The Importance of Developing Home Language and Cultural Competence

For young children, cultural and linguistic identity constitutes an essential part of a sense of self and belonging. Knowing the family language facilitates cultural learning, smooth emotional communication, and the establishment of the relationship between teachers and families in early care settings, which in turn contributes to the well-being of the entire family (Kouritzin 1999; Shin 2005; Wong-Fillmore 1991). Contrary to what some might believe, children are highly capable of learning two languages at the same time, and the growth in one supports the growth of the other. Children who have strong home language skills tend to transition more smoothly to proficiency in English (Cummins 1991). Children who are dual-language learners may also enjoy cognitive advantages, such as showing earlier abilities to understand words as symbols for meanings, and stronger abilities to focus by inhibiting irrelevant stimulation (Bialystok 1999; Hilchey and Klein 2011).

Communication and Language Development in Non-English-Speaking-Homes

Like children who are monolingual, an infant or toddler who has been exposed to more than one language has had rich language and social experiences before coming to care. For children who learn two languages at the same time (simultaneous dual-language learners), the number of words they know in each language is usually fewer than that of their monolingual peers *when vocabulary sizes are counted separately in each of their two languages.* However, *when the words that simultaneous dual-language learners know are added together,* research shows they know at least the same number of words as their monolingual peers, if not more. A child's relative competence in each language is directly related to the amount of input they receive in each language, with higher frequency and diversity of vocabulary words related to higher competence (Pearson, Fernández, and Oiler 1993; Hoff et al. 2011). When an infant/toddler program gives children experience with English and is unable to provide input in a child's home language,

it is important for the program to convey to families the benefit of continuing to communicate with their infants and toddlers in the home language. That way the children will receive higher frequency and diversity of language input in both their home language and English through their cumulative experiences in their home and early care setting.

Whether learning one language or two languages, infants and toddlers rely greatly on nonverbal means—such as face-to-face contact, gestures, posture, and body contact—to communicate with their caregivers. As an adaptation to their specific social and community life demands, different nonverbal communication styles have evolved in various cultural communities. In some cultural communities, for instance, caregivers engage infants in much more face-to-face contact than body contact. This practice often reflects caregivers' beliefs of infants as autonomous beings with their own

intentions, emotions, and preferences to be attended to primarily though eye-to-eye gaze (Keller et al. 2010).

In other cultural communities, caregivers engage infants in much more body contact than face-to-face interactions. Infants are carried on the caregivers' back, hip, and in the front facing away from the caregivers. Such extensive body contact conveys to infants a sense of warmth, feelings of relatedness, and belongingness. It also fosters the development of caregiver–child mutual sensitivity through body language such as gestures and postural changes. The reliance on body language makes verbal communication and face-to-face interaction less prevalent. For example, a parent may direct a child, solely through gestures without any verbal input, to solve a problem. Such practices often reflect caregivers' beliefs that body contact establishes effective communication, as well as their goal to socialize children into an integral part of the family and community. To support children who are dual-language learners, programs need to become aware of both verbal and nonverbal communication styles specific to the cultural communities of the children. Continuity between home and the early care setting for infants and toddlers learning a second language involves respect for culturally based ways of communicating. Collaborating with the family is essential to learning about an infant's or toddler's experiences with nonverbal communication at home.

Strategies for Creating Collaborative, Reciprocal Relationships with Linguistically Diverse Families

Create collaborative and reciprocal relationships with linguistically diverse families through some strategies that are generally used with all families (no matter their language background) and some that are unique to dual-language learners and families with a home language other than English. When infant/toddler care teachers use general strategies to work together with families, communication can be in any language—their common language or through interpretation. The PITC resource *Infant/Toddler Caregiving: A Guide to Creating Partnerships with Families* (CDE 2010) provides many useful strategies. Those strategies are expanded below to consider the additional factor of use of multiple languages.

Establish clear two-way communication with the family

Learn what is going on at home:

- Express interest in a child's home language by asking about the language, such as where it is spoken, whether there are different dialects, what the written symbols look like, what nonverbal interaction with young infants is like.

- Inquire about how the child communicates at home with caregivers. Gain a sense of the English abilities of the different caregivers and who speaks what language in what amount to the child.

- Inquire about parents' goals for child's cultural learning and language development.

Communicate with the family about what is going on in the early care setting:

- Explain that the care program has adopted the philosophy of support for bicultural and bilingual development of children, an approach for the long-term good of the child and the family.

- If teachers have previously encountered children from non-English speaking homes and the program has developed certain practices, explain to parents how infant care teachers typically interact and communicate with children from homes where another language is spoken. Communicate to the family members that the teachers will seek to learn common phrases in the home language, particularly around care routines. Seek family members' responses and suggestions.

- Explain to families, that for babies and young toddlers, it is beneficial to have a primary infant care teacher who speaks the child's language and that, whenever possible, the child will be cared for by a provider who shares the same home language and/or cultural heritage. Cultural and linguistic continuity strengthens the child's developing identity and offers the child a comfortable and familiar base of security, both essential for learning and development in all domains. Explain that if it is not possible to provide a child with a teacher who speaks the child's home language and/ or shares the home cultural heritage, the child's home language will be supported. The primary care teacher will learn some common phrases in the home language, particularly around care routines. Seek family members' responses and suggestions.

- If a child coming to the program is one of the first with a non-English-speaking background, discuss with family members the program's proposed plans and seek feedback and suggestions.

- Describe to family members what kind of resources the early care setting has to provide support in the child's

home language (e.g., the presence or absence of infant/toddler care teachers who can speak the child's home language).

Collaborate with families to support a child's bicultural and bilingual language development

Infant/toddler care teachers and family members should work together on strategies to be used at home:

- Encourage family members to continue to speak to the child in the home language. Entering an English-speaking care setting may be a turning point for language development for many children.* Some families are eager for

---

*If family members report that their children will reply only in English or are obviously uninterested in their home language—even when the family continues to use the home language—encourage family members to keep using the home language. That way, children will receive ongoing exposure to the home language and can continue to improve their listening skills.

their children to quickly fit into the new environment and think learning English as quickly as possible is the most effective strategy. Family members who know English often switch to using English at home to "facilitate" this language transition. It is only when their children are firmly on track for English a year or two down the road and refuse to speak to them in their home language that they realize that it is difficult to turn back to it (Shin 2005).

- Support family members in keeping the child interested in the home language.

Explain that children who have continuous exposure to their home language for many years by listening to and speaking it at home do not all develop strong proficiency in their home language. Those whose home language use is confined to household routines, in the long run, may end up with a limited vocabulary and cannot talk about things that are unfamiliar and beyond their comfort zone. However, those who are supported to use their home language beyond home (e.g., interactions with members of the community who share the same language), and at home beyond household routines (e.g., being read to in home language) develop strong long-term home language skills. Help families appreciate the importance of a rich home-language experience. In some cases, families may be more aware of these strategies than teachers and are already actively practicing these strategies. In that case, infant and toddler care teachers can turn family–teacher communication into opportunities to learn from the families.

- Encourage family members to recount family and cultural stories with their children in their home language.

Encourage families to read interesting and age-appropriate books to their children in their home language (when available). Help families to discover places (e.g., libraries, bookstores, online stores) and people (e.g., relatives coming from the home country for a visit) that can provide language rich experiences. When books in the home language are not easily available, guide parents to use English books but spontaneously translate them into their home language for children. Recommend family members to talk with their children above and beyond book reading. Storytelling and conversing are activities that all families do naturally and require no additional resources. This recommendation is particularly important for families from cultures in which family members see reading more as a learning experience than as a form of entertainment.

- Encourage family members to support parent–child interactions or child play by providing rich language input, such as naming the texture, smell and taste of the food a child is eating; describing how a child is playing with a toy; or how the child is feeling. Advocate families to share family stories and jointly retell shared experiences with children. Suggest that families ask open-ended questions and ask their children to describe actions, processes, and events. Encourage family members to challenge themselves to use a richer vocabulary than they normally would use in daily life or than they would normally assume is natural for interacting with young children. Reiterate that the family is the main and often sole source of children's home language input, a situation different from that of children living in their home country. Explain the importance of the adult paying attention to things that the child is interested in as a way to create meaningful language contexts.

- Encourage immediate family members to help children maintain close ties to extended family members, friends, and other individuals in the home language and culture community. Encourage families to develop relationships with other families with the same cultural and/or language backgrounds who share some of the same developmental goals. Regular interactions with others who share their home language or are a part of their cultural community enhance culture and language learning outcomes for children, helping children see the relevance of their language and culture to the larger community.

- Invite family members to support teachers in efforts to enhance home

language and culture presence at the program.

a. Invite family members to bring to class audio and visual materials and books for children in the home language and share them with the child individually or with a group of children.

b. Encourage family members to speak to their children in their home language during drop-off and pickup or other times when they are at the program; show interest when that is going on, and praise or acknowledge the effort when children respond to parents in the home language. These behaviors provide cues for children that their home language is valued in the early care setting.

c. Invite parents and other family members to the child care program to lead activities that express elements of home language and culture. For example, one program

asked a mother to show staff members how babies in her culture are swaddled in a certain way and why. Another program asked visiting grandparents from their home country to read to children a book in their home language.

Be sensitive to how you communicate with children

- Infants and toddlers are attentive and sensitive to nonverbal communication cues, such as facial expressions, gestures, and eye-gaze. Teachers should consistently maintain a communication style that is regarded as beneficial for all children—a style that is responsive, warm, patient, and clear. However, as teachers learn from families' about their children's communication styles at home, that information should be taken into account when communicating with children in the early care setting.

- In accord with PITC practices that aim to support the child's home language and cultural competence, teachers who can speak the child's home language should use the home language for communication.

- "English-speaking caregivers should never fear that English is bad and should not hesitate to speak to the child as they would to infants from their own language" (Garcia 1991, 6). Infants and toddlers have remarkable abilities to distinguish between two languages and to pick up a new language. Speaking to them in English in the care setting lays a foundation for their English-language development. Doing this will not take away children's opportunities to learn their home language if no teachers can speak the child's home language, and children continue to have strong support in the home language as suggested before.

- Together with family members, come up with solutions for the basic routines related to language used for social purposes.

  a. How to address each other: Families from some cultures may not feel comfortable addressing the teachers by first name. Families who speak nonalphabetic languages may find the names of the teachers and other parents and children hard to remember. Some mutually agreed upon ways of addressing each other should be decided. Sheets with teachers' and children's names (with pronunciations marked) can be distributed to the caregivers.

  b. Home language phrases: At entry to the program, have families fill

out a form that asks how to say, in the child's home language, common phrases, such as "You want this?" "Come to me," "Here you are," "Good job," and "Snack time." Teachers can then memorize these phrases (or keep the sheet handy to refer to until they do learn them) and use them with the child, sandwiched with English phrases.

  c. Dialogue book: Keep a dialogue book to communicate with families. Teachers may jot notes in the book about the individual child throughout the day, as well as comments or messages to the parents. The family members can then take the dialogue book home, read the comments, or have someone translate them, and respond to the teacher after taking some time to reflect on the messages. The teacher and family members can then refer back to previous comments as they think about the child's development and progress. Such communication has several advantages. Some family members can read English better than they can speak it. The written form of communication takes advantage of their stronger areas of English. For family members who also cannot read English well, written communication is a record that they can take and ask other people to translate. Written communication also gives families more time to think through what the teacher has shared with them.

  d. Photo documentation: Take photos of children engaging in different activities throughout the day. When family members arrive to pick up the child, the teachers can hand them the camera and show them some pictures so that family members have a better idea of what the child did. Photos can also be used to help reinforce different messages or suggested strategies for families to use at home.

e. Home language and cultural support network: Identify and establish a network of individuals who share the child's home language and culture. Involve both teachers and family members in this network. It may consist of individuals from other families in the same program, families in other programs, teachers in a different class but in the same program, teachers in another program, a friend or relative of the child's family, an older sibling or an older bilingual child in the program (only for age-appropriate content). Such a network provides support in language translation to the early care program whenever necessary. To the involved families, the network helps provide a resource for sharing information and also a place to get help or support. One early care program has reported

that families who are able to connect with some sort of social or support network are able to connect in more meaningful ways with the teachers. It is particularly important to begin to establish the network before a family enrolls so that families receive support right from the beginning. Maintain the network as an ongoing project and share the resources with other programs.

f. Translating written materials: Routine and formal information about a program should be translated into languages present at the program. Multiple programs can share such resources.

Conclusion

Infants and toddlers from homes where English is not the dominant language bring to early care settings rich experiences—some that are universal and some that are unique. Families in North America aspire for their children to be fully integrated into North American society and have adopted child-rearing goals and practices deemed to be optimal. However, as the goals and practices that families engage in are derived from families' culturally specific knowledge and experiences, some goals and practices may differ from those that teachers are familiar with. The first step toward collaborative, reciprocal relationships with families is to identify, understand, and appreciate those experiences.

The second step in developing collaborative, reciprocal relationships with families is to work together at utilizing strategies to support their children's development and learning. One set of strategies involves building connections between children's home language and culture and their experiences in the infant/toddler care program to foster the overall development of children. The other set of strategies is to support the development of bilingual language skills that will, in turn, benefit the overall development of children. Through collaborative relationships, infant/toddler care teachers have an opportunity to learn together with families and help their children to gain the full benefits of learning two languages early in life.

References

Bialystok, E. 1999. "Cognitive Complexity and Attentional Control in the Bilingual Mind." *Child Development* 70:636–44.

California Department of Education (CDE). 2010. *Infant/Toddler Caregiving: A Guide to Creating Partnerships with Families.* 2nd ed. Sacramento: CDE.

Cummins, J. 1991. "Interdependence of First- and Second-Language Proficiency in Bilingual Children." In *Language Processing in Bilingual Children,* edited by E. Bialystok. Cambridge, MA: Cambridge University Press.

Garcia, E. E. 1991. "Caring for Infants in a Bilingual Child Care Setting." *The Journal of Educational Issues of Language Minority Students* 9:1–10.

Hammer, C. S., G. Jia, and Y. Uchikoshi. 2011. "Language and Literacy Development of Dual Language Learners Growing Up in the United States: A Call for Research." *Child Development Perspectives* 5 (1): 4–9.

Hilchey, M. D., and R. M. Klein. 2011. "Are There Bilingual Advantages on Nonlinguistic Interference Tasks? Implications for the Plasticity of Executive Control Processes." *Psychonomic Bulletin & Review* 18 (4): 625–58.

Hoff, E., C. Core, S. Place, R. Rumiche, M. Señor, and M. Parra 2011. Dual Language Exposure and Early Bilingual Development." *Journal of Child Language* 39:1–27.

Keller, H., J. Borke,, B. Lamm, A. Lohaus, and R. D. Yovsi. 2010. "Developing Patterns of Parenting in Two Cultural Communities." *International Journal of Behavioral Development* 35 (3): 233–45.

Keller, H., R. D. Yovsi, J. Borke, J. Kärtner, H. Jensen, and Z. Papaligoura. 2004. "Developmental Consequences of Early Parenting Experiences: Self-Recognition and Self-Regulation in Three Cultural Communities." *Child Development* 75:1745–60.

Kouritzin, S. G. 1999. *Facets of First Language Loss.* Mahwah, NJ: Lawrence Erlbaum Associates.

Pearson, B. Z., S. C. Fernandez, and D. K. Oiler. 1993. "Lexical Development in Bilingual Infants and Toddlers: Comparison to Monolingual Norms." *Language Learning* 43:93–120.

Rogoff, B. 2003. *The Cultural Nature of Human Development.* New York: Oxford University Press.

Shin, S. J. 2005. *Developing in Two Languages: Korean Children in America.* Tonawanda, NY: Multilingual Matters Ltd.

Wong Fillmore, L. 1991. "When Learning a Second Language Means Losing the First." *Early Childhood Research Quarterly* 6:323–46.

Section Four

Suggested Resources

Books

Barrera, I., and R. Corso. 2003. *Skilled Dialogue: Strategies for Responding to Cultural Diversity in Early Childhood.* Baltimore, MD: Paul H. Brookes.

Barrera, I., and L. Kramer. 2009. *Using Skilled Dialogue to Transform Challenging Interactions. Honoring Identity, Voice, and Connection.* Baltimore, MD: Paul H. Brookes.

Brody, H. 2000. *The Other Side of Eden: Hunters, Farmers, and the Shaping of the World.* New York: North Point Press.

Castro, D. C., B. Ayankoya, and C. Kasprzak. 2011a. *New Voices/Nuevas Voces: Guide to Cultural and Linguistic Diversity in Early Childhood Handbook.* Baltimore, MD: Paul H. Brookes.

———. 2011b. *New Voices/Nuevas Voces: Facilitator's Guide to Cultural and Linguistic Diversity in Early Childhood.* CD-ROM. Baltimore, MD: Paul H. Brookes.

Chen, D., M. D. Klein, and A. V. Osipova. 2012. "Two Is Better than One! In Defense of Home Language Maintenance and Bilingualism for Young Dual Language Learners with Disabilities." In *Supporting Young Children Who Are Dual Language Learners with or at Risk for Disabilities. Young Exceptional Children* Monograph Series No. 14. Longmont, CO: Sopris West.

Chen, D., M. McLean, R. M. Corso, and D. Bruns. 2005. "Working Together in Early Intervention: Cultural Considerations in Helping Relationships and Service Utilization." In *Building Healthy Relationships with Families,* edited by R. M. Corso, S. A. Fowler, and R. M. Santos, 39–58. Longmont, CO: Sopris West.

Day, M., and R. Parlakian. 2004. *How Culture Shapes Social–Emotional Development. Implications for Practice in Infant-Family Programs.* Washington, DC: Zero to Three.

Fadiman, A. 1997. *The Spirit Catches You and You Fall Down: A Hmong Child, Her American Doctors and the Collision of Two Cultures.* New York: Farrar, Straus and Giroux.

Gonzalez-Mena, J. 2008. *Diversity in Early Care and Education: Honoring Differences.* Washington, DC: National Association for the Education of Young Children.

———. 2013. *50 Strategies for Working and Communicating with Diverse Families.* 3rd ed. Upper Saddle River, NJ: Pearson.

Howes, C., R. C. Pianta, and J. T. Downer, eds. 2011. *Dual Language Learners in the Early Childhood Classroom.* Baltimore, MD: Paul H. Brookes.

Jacobson, T. 2003. *Confronting Our Discomforts: Clearing the Way for Anti-bias in Early Childhood.* Portsmouth, NH: Heinemann.

Keyser, J. 2006. *From Parents to Partners: Building a Family-Centered Early Childhood Program.* St. Paul, MN: Redleaf Press; and Washington, DC: National Association for the Education of Young Children.

Lynch, E. W., and M. J. Hanson. 2011. *Developing Cross-Cultural Competence: A Guide for Working with Children and Their Families.* 4th. ed. Baltimore, MD: Paul H. Brookes.

Nemeth, K. N. 2009. *Many Languages, One Classroom: Teaching English Language Learners.* Silver Spring, MD: Gryphon House.

———. 2012. *Many Languages, Building Connections: Supporting Infants and Toddler Who Are Dual Language Learners.* Lewisville, NC: Gryphon House.

Parlakian, R. 2003. *How Culture Shapes Social-Emotional Development: Implications for Practice in Infant-Family Programs.* Washington, DC: Zero to Three: National Center for Infants, Toddlers & Families.

Rogoff, B. 2003. *The Cultural Nature of Human Development.* New York: Oxford University Press.

Santos, R. M., G. R. Cheatham, and L. Duran, eds. 2012. *Young Exceptional Children Monograph Series No. 14: Supporting Young Children Who Are Dual Language Learners with or at Risk for Disabilities.* Longmont, CO: Sopris West.

Small, M. 1998. *Our Babies, Ourselves: How Biology and Culture Shape the Way We Parent.* New York: Random House.

Tabors, P. O. 2008. *One Child, Two Languages: A Guide for Early Childhood Educators of Children Learning English as a Second Language.* 2nd ed. Baltimore, MD: Paul H. Brookes.

Articles

Bronson, P., and A. Merryman. 2009. "See Baby Discriminate." *Newsweek* (September 14): 53–59.

Denney, M. K., T. Itkonen, and Y. Okamoto. 2007. "Early Intervention Systems of Care for Latino Families and Their Young Children with Special Needs: Salient Themes and Guiding Implications." *Infants & Young Children* 30: 326–35.

Division for Early Childhood (DEC). 2010. "Responsiveness to ALL Children, Families, and Professionals: Integrating Cultural and Linguistic Diversity into Policy and Practice." DEC position statement. Missoula, MT: The Division for Early Childhood. http://www.dec-sped.org/.

Espinosa, L. M. 2008. *Challenging Common Myths About Young English Language Learners (Policy Brief No. 8).* New York: Foundation for Child Development. http://fcd-us.org/.

Garcia, S. B., A. M. Perez, and A. A. Ortiz. 2000. Interpreting Mexican-American Mothers' Beliefs About Language Disabilities from a Sociocultural Perspective: Implications for Early Childhood Intervention." *Remedial and Special Education* 21 (2): 90–100, 120.

Genesee, F. 2008. "Early Dual Language Learning." *Zero to Three* (September 2008): 17–23.

Gonzalez-Mena, J. 2010. "Cultural Responsiveness and Routines: When Center and Home Don't Match." *Exchange* 32 (3): 42–44.

Gonzalez-Mena, J., and D. Widmeyer Eyer. 2012. *Infants, Toddlers and Caregivers.* 9th ed. New York: McGraw-Hill.

Im, J., R. Parlakian, and S. Sanchez. 2007. "Supporting Infants, Toddlers and Their Families: Understanding the Influence of Culture on Caregiving Practices from the Inside Out." *Young Children* 62 (5): 65–66.

Jackson, C. W., L. Leacox, and M. F. Callender. 2010. "Challenges to Early Intervention for English Language Learners." *Early Childhood Services* 2: 29–53.

Lee, H., M. M. Ostrosky, T. Bennett, and S. A. Fowler. 2003. "Perspectives of Early Intervention Professionals About Culturally-Appropriate Practices." *Journal of Early Intervention* 25: 281–95.

National Association for the Education of Young Children (NAEYC). 1995. "Responding to Linguistic and Cultural Diversity: Recommendations for Effective Early Childhood Education." Position Statement. Washington, DC: NAEYC. http://www.naeyc.org (accessed November 19, 2012).

Ohtake, Y., R. M. Santos, and S. A. Fowler. 2000. "It's a Three-Way Conversation: Families, Service Providers, and Interpreters Working Together." *Young Exceptional Children* 4 (1): 12–18.

Perez, A. M. 2000. "Mexican American Mothers' Perceptions and Beliefs About Language Acquisition in Infants and Toddlers with Disabilities." *Bilingual Research Journal* 24 (3): 1–15.

Puig, V. I. 2010. "Are Early Intervention Services Replacing Home Languages and Cultures 'at Risk'? *Early Childhood Research & Practice* 12 (1): 1–19. http://ecrp.uiuc.edu/v12n1/puig.html (accessed November 19, 2012).

Zepeda, M., J. Gonzalez-Mena, C. Rothstein-Fisch, and E. Trumbull. 2006. *Bridging Cultures in Early Care and Education: A Training Module.* San Francisco: WestEd.

Zero to Three. 2008. "Language, Culture, and Learning." *Zero to Three* 29 (1).

Videos/DVDs

California Department of Education. 2007. *A World Full of Language: Supporting Preschool English Learners.* Sacramento: California Department of Education. DVD.

Chen, D., M. Haney, and A. Cox. 2012. *Supporting Cultural and Linguistic Diversity in Early Intervention and Early Childhood Special Education: A Cross-Cultural Competence Video Library.* DVD. Baltimore, MD: Paul H. Brookes.

Educational Productions. 2002. *Starting Points: For Educators of Culturally and Linguistically Diverse Young Children.*

Program 1: I Don't Know Where to Start

Program 2: Getting Your Message Across

Program 3: Bringing Language Alive!

Online Resources

Center for Early Care and Education Research: Dual Language Learners (CECER-DLL). http://www.cecerdll.fpg. unc.edu/ (accessed November 19, 2012).

Culturally and Linguistically Appropriate Services (CLAS)—Early Childhood Research Institute. http://www.clas. uiuc.edu/ (accessed November 19, 2012).

Early Childhood Technical Assistance (ECTA) Center. http://ectacenter.org/ (accessed April 3, 2013).

National Association for Bilingual Education (NABE). http://www.nabe.org/ (accessed April 3, 2013).

National Center for Cultural Competence (Georgetown University Center for Child and Human Development). http://www11.georgetown.edu/research/ gucchd/nccc/ (accessed November 19, 2012).

OSP 13 131071   12-004 PR12-0015 6-13 10M